We would like to dedicate this play to the many children and young people who have lost their lives to organised crime and criminal child exploitation in the 21st century. The first child lost was a child too many.

Natalia & Phil

Foreword from the authors

This is a play, over four acts, that depicts a threatening world of criminal and subversive behaviour which targets children and young people.

It looks at the world from the perspective of a modern teenager. It is not a 'true story' – but the events within this depiction are both realistic and honest. We have woven together many strands from the stories and experiences of very real people.

We strive to provide you – as our audience – with a journey through this world. It is a world that is not hidden from view, but it is rarely acknowledged. If we are not wilfully blind to this place – which lives in most communities now – we are all guilty of being equally short sighted at various times.

This play comes with a genuine warning – it deals with adult themes applied to immature and adolescent protagonists. As a consequence, this can be distressing for the viewer.

There is adult language – this is a reflection of the language that is being used on the streets. It is not used for gratuitous purposes; it is considered a part of the accurate portrayal of this world and it is retained only for valid artistic reasons. We are striving for accuracy and authenticity and our experiments with alternative vocabulary have so far severely undermined the quality of what we have sought to deliver. To this end, what you are about to see is, at times, quite uncompromising.

The overarching purpose of this play is didactic - that is to say we are not merely seeking to entertain or move you emotionally, we are also seeking to instruct, to present a reasoned argument, and we are seeking to educate.

For all of these reasons, if you are an adult with children, we advise that *young children* do not attend this play - and if they do attend that you accept responsibility for what they might observe and what they might hear. Opinions on whether older children and young adolescents should see this play will vary. There are violent themes, there are overt sexual references, there is abusive language and (without apology) the events are impactful, distressing and alarming.

Natalia Huckle & Phil Priestley

TRIGGER WARNING

This play contains overt references to, and the portrayal of:

- Domestic Abuse

- Sexual Abuse

- Drink Spiking

- Knife Crime & Serious Street Based Violence

- Unplanned pregnancy and overt references to sex

- Drug & Alcohol Misuse

- Self-Harm

- Organised Crime & the Exploitation of Children

- Non-specific Religious Imagery & References

- Vomiting

The Cast

(in order of appearance)

Eli	
Brown	
Charlie	
The Devil (he/him)	
Teenager 1 (he/him)	
Young Persons Worker	
Cara	
Teacher (he/him)	
Maya	
Jack	
Lucy	
Dani	
Aiden	

Granddad	
VOICE: Cara's Mum (Professor Walker)	
VOICE: Cara's Dad (Mr Walker)	
The Angel (she/her)	
Jon	
Tom	
Boomer (the dog)	
Girl 1	
Junior	
PC Wilson	
PC Clarke	
VOICE: Voicemail	
Care Home Worker	
The Boss	

Junior Doctor	
Local Politician	
National Politician	
Social Care Manager	
Senior Police Officer	

Act 1

Act 1
Scene I: *A Church Yard*

Eli (a 14-year-old boy dressed unassumingly in his school uniform with a hoodie thrown over the top) sits amongst the audience. We don't notice him at first until a phone starts ringing loudly. It's his. He grabs it from his pocket and answers it hastily and with a bit of a fumble.

Eli   Hello? Yeah I know it's late but I said I'd be home in a bit. *[Looking around, preoccupied, nervous laugh]* Mum's always mad.

Eli stands up and begins walking through the audience towards the stage, looking behind him suspiciously with each step. The stage is dressed to resemble an abandoned graveyard: dark and grimy with several gravestones punctuating the background. One of them reads: 'Aiden Ramsey'. It is newer, fresher and is adorned with teddy bears, flowers and cards.

Eli   Tell her I'm just leaving Hannah's house, so I'll literally be 15 minutes tops. *[agitated]* Yes, I'll eat it cold, just leave it on the table. Okay. Yep. Bye.

Eli is on the stage now. Three foreboding figures emerge out of the darkness. We come to know them later as Charlie, Brown and the Devil. Eli approaches them nervously.

Brown   Alright?

Eli   Yeah… I called before… you said we could meet here? That you *might* be able to er… sort me out?

Charlie   Maybe, what do you need?

Eli   *[Loudly]* Oh I thought I said! Some coke?

Charlie   Shhh kid what are you with the fucking cops? Jesus!

Brown   Where are your mates?

Eli   They… er… backed out. I've… I've got the money you asked for - all of it - it's all here…

Eli produces an amount of money. It's in notes and change but as he pulls out from his pocket, the change is dropped and coins clatter loudly as they hit the stage floor. Eli immediately falls to his knees, looking to gather it all up so that they don't think he has short-changed them…

The men look at each other and roll their eyes like 'what the hell is this supposed to be'.

Eli reaches out to Brown with several of the notes he has managed to pick up in his hand whilst carrying looking for the rest of the change.

Brown   *[Unimpressed]* This ain't the corner shop son.

Eli   *[flustered]* I know...sorry...I

Charlie   [Interrupts] You see it's like this. It's getting dark, and we're very busy. We have customers, loyal customers and we don't have time for snivelling rats like you. Explain to me why the hell we need to give you anything in return for this shit that you call money?

Eli   [Confused] What? But I...

The Devil whispers to Brown – who immediately grabs Eli, hard, by the throat. He lifts him onto the tips of his toes and stares him deep in the eyes. Eli urinates himself. Charlie then punches Eli in the stomach, who doubles over – coughing and gasping. Eli sinks slowly to the ground. Brown then grabs hold of Eli and man-handles him deeper into the church yard so that he is eventually obscured from the audience's view by a wall. Brown and Charlie then work him over with punches and kicks while the Devil appears to act as a look out: standing slightly in view of the audience, seemingly unaffected by what is going on behind him. The audience should be protected from seeing the physical impact of the blows by the wall and gravestones in the church yard.

Eli [Coughing and sobbing] Stop! Please, I won't tell anyone, I promise. I'm sorry, please...

The Devil whispers to Brown again. Brown grabs Eli by his ankles and drags him off stage. When the three gang members reappear from the wings of the stage they have Eli's clothing, his phone, his wallet and his school bag. Charlie throws the school trousers at Brown, laughing. Brown throws them aside.

Brown   Ugh! What do I need pissy school trousers for?

They laugh as if the enormity and destructiveness of what they have just done means nothing to them. They walk down off the stage and exit the theatre along the central gangway to the rear. Charlie continues laughing at Brown whilst Brown shakes his head and wipes his hands on his trousers. The Devil doesn't go with them – he exits in a different direction.

[Song 1: Opening number]

Act 1

Scene II: *Support Group*

Eli, now in a fresh school uniform, sits glumly in a chair at the front of the stage. Ten or so teenagers, including Cara and Dani – whose stories are introduced later on, are sat around him. They are arranged roughly in the shape of a semicircle. A Young Person's Worker is leading the group and stands to the side. Eli is trying to keep his composure, but he is shaking as he re-tells what happened to him:

Eli   I don't even know who they were...they told me that...I had the money and everything...I don't know what I did...they took me to the back of the graveyard by the wood so that nobody would see. They just kept kicking and punching, they spat on me, I didn't think they were gonna stop until...then they took everything that I had...everything... my money, my phone...my...my...

Eli looks down at his blazer and crosses his arms over his chest as he remembers himself naked

Eli   After they'd taken everything, they went further. One guy went further. I thought he was just gonna beat me up again...but...he did *things* to me... he...

Eli's words fail him, and his face is blank. He stares off into the distance. He can't talk anymore. Teenager 1 shakes his head.

Eli   Yeah

The Young Person's Worker awkwardly intervenes on this incredibly difficult moment that seems to hang in the air between everyone

Young Persons Worker   Okay. Thank you for sharing that, Eli. That can't have been easy. If you guys need it, we can take a break, but we have a couple more people who still haven't spoken. Cara, you up for it today?

Cara is sat – arms folded, legs crossed, hood up – hunched over in her seat, trying desperately not to be noticed. Her stomach is heavily bandaged. Everyone in the group turns simultaneously and rather melodramatically to look at her. She looks up and scowls.

Young Persons Worker	*[speaks intimately with Cara]* Come on sweet. Some people have shared some really personal things today. Isn't it time they know a little bit about what happened to you? It's why you're here, isn't it?

There is a long, uncomfortable silence. Eventually, Cara reluctantly stands up and swaps seats with Eli.

Cara	Fine. [long pause] But before I start, I just want to say that I wasn't always like 'this'. So please don't judge me. I didn't…I didn't grow up in places where there were knives

hidden under mattresses or ...or packets of pills stuffed under kitchen sinks. I had a 'normal' life.

As Cara talks, the support group setting dissolves and a Secondary School classroom is set up around her. Several students including Jack, Maya, Dani, Lucy, Eli and the Devil sit at desks either side of her or behind her. A desk with a Bunsen Burner, boiling tube, clamp and textbook is placed in front of her. Cara remains in exactly the same position and seems to be unaware of the changing setting. We're in her story now. As she's talking, her tone grows angry and resentful.

Cara You don't notice how quickly you get sucked into it all. You know, I used to have sleepovers and birthday parties. I used to build a snowman whenever it snowed. I used to see Granddad every day and we would and sing and dance and look at his photographs. Normal things. God, it sounds so pathetic. So pathetic and… *[pause]* perfect. *[Shouting]* So don't you dare judge me! *[Quietly with composure once again]* They're childish things really but... I am a child...I mean...I was...I am. I used to do everything before this world

became everything I'd got and
I wasn't allowed the time or
the permission from the people
who owned me. I used to be
good at stuff too – *besides
lying and getting laid*. I
guess you forget about that.

Cara then looks away from us, pulls her top down over the bloody bandage and begins fiddling with the Bunsen burner and the boiling tube set up in front of her. Now Cara is transported back in time to just before her nightmare began. She looks fresh, she is uninjured, and she has none of the non-verbal behaviours that indicate a post-traumatic struggle with mental health. The Teacher, who has been walking up and down between the desks during Cara's monologue, stops to look at Cara's setup.

Teacher   That's right Cara - excellent! Did everyone see what Cara did there? I want it just like Cara does it. That is so good. Just like that.

Cara blushes. Several classmates begin whispering all the typical, shallow insults that people who raise their hand in lessons get, behind Cara's back ("try-hard", "nerd", "teacher's pet" etc.). There are smirks of jealousy as the teacher praises Cara. Cara is very academic and has always been particularly good at science and her peers use this as an opportunity to undermine and ridicule her.

Maya   Oooh the try-hard is at it again guys – I bet you do it how all the teachers like it, isn't that right Cara?

Sniggers ripple throughout the class.

Jack   Oi Maya, leave her alone you cow. Cara is just… eager to please, that's all.

Jack smirks at Maya

Teacher   Settle down.

The school bell rings to signal the end of the day and all the students begin to pack up their things, making lots of noise as the Teacher tries to talk over them.

Teacher   (shouting) The bell is for me not for you!

As he says these words, Jack mouths them behind him in perfect timing.

Teacher Right, don't forget homework on ionic bonding is due tomorrow and I expect a full hypothesis and method for the required practical we did in class today, emailed to me by Monday morning otherwise you'll be spending lunchtime with me and trust me I'm sure both you and I can think of much better ways to occupy our time. So please, for the love of God, don't be that person!

Maya *[To Lucy]* Cara can't – I bet she'd love ionic bondage with him at lunch…

Several of Maya's friends laugh, including Jack. The class begins to file out of the classroom

Teacher   Oh, and Cara, can you stay behind for a moment please?

Several of the class, including Maya, Lucy, Dani and Jack let out a derisive "Ooooooh" before sniggering and leaving the room. The Teacher doesn't hear any of this - or chooses to ignore it adeptly - and begins walking around the desks picking up books whilst talking to Cara.

Teacher   Cara, the work I have seen from you – particularly today and over the last few weeks – has been *really* impressive. I think you have a real gift for chemistry – and your other teachers think that you are highly capable too. Have you thought about what college you want to apply to yet? The deadline is coming up isn't it?

Cara   Well, I really want to go to the Sandford Institute of Science and Technology – but I didn't think I'd get in…

Teacher   What are you talking about? You'd definitely get in - in fact - I was wondering whether you'd consider letting me help you to apply for a scholarship there?

Cara   Really? Are you serious?

Teacher   You've got the talent. You could really do something amazing one day if you push yourself forward.

Cara   Thanks Sir.

Teacher   Now go on - get out of here!

Cara smiles at her teacher before gathering up her belongings and leaving the classroom. In the corridor, Cara is met by Maya and several of her 'pack' – including Lucy and Dani

Maya   *[high pitched mocking voice]*
"OOH CARA YOU'RE SO TALENTED"

They all laugh in chorus. They've been listening through the door. Cara attempts to walk away but is encircled by the group.

Cara   Leave off Maya – haven't you got some year 7's head to flush down the toilet or something?

Maya   [Mock sadness] Wow. That hurts. You cut me deep... Shrek.

Cara grows frustrated and attempts to push past two of the girls. One of them gasps.

Lucy   Oh my God! She just touched me!

Dani   No way. Did you just touch my best friend?

Dani attempts to square up to Cara

Cara   Give it a rest

Maya   Seriously Cara, you're gonna get it for that

Maya moves closer to Cara so that their noses are almost touching. She runs the knuckle of her right index finger down the side of Cara's face, firmly but with faux admiration

Maya [looking Cara up and down] You're so pretty you know. So pretty. And I do like pretty things...I wouldn't want anything to spoil that pretty face. But sadly, I can't say the same for any of my other girls. So, watch your back Cara 'cos nobody likes a know it all…

[Song 2: Acapella rap sequence]

The girl group crow and congratulate each other "Oooooh burn" etc.

Maya walks away, her group follows her. Cara is almost boiling over with anger, but she feels simultaneously disempowered and crushed by what just happened. Overwhelmed with anxiety, she begins to hyperventilate before running off stage to vomit in the wings. She then walks back onto the front of the stage whilst wiping her mouth, and sits down, her feet hanging over the edge. Aiden who has been watching all this happen at a distance tries to approach Cara - he is obviously nervous.

Aiden   You okay Cara?

As Aiden gets closer to Cara, Jack runs from the back of the stage and violently pushes past Aiden to sit down confidently next to Cara. Cara appears not to have heard Aiden - or may have mistaken the call to have come from Jack. Aiden swallows his moment of confidence and redirects himself off the stage feeling embarrassed that he tried and failed to talk to her.

Jack   Heyy Babe!

Jack puts his arm around Cara. Cara shakes him off. Jack has been flirting with her - and this is not attention she has been seeking. He just keeps finding her. Jack is a very popular boy. He is a ringleader and most of the girls fancy him even if they don't like themselves for it. Cara feels like this.

Cara   [*Resentfully*] Don't patronise me. I'm honestly not in the mood for this.

Jack   [mockingly] Alright, alright, my bad! [*Pause*] But you just don't get it do you?

There is a pregnant pause between them – Cara looks at him like "Well what?"

Jack   [serious tone] Ok, ok... [*dramatic pause*] it's always been you.

Cara   Oh *piss off* Jack

She shoves him and Jack stands up, laughing

[Song 3: Jack's Song]

Jack How can you not even know that, like, every boy in this school secretly loves you, Cara? I can't even. I ain't mocking you like when are you are gonna be fair to me. When are you gonna take me seriously?

Cara When you start being serious.

Cara stands up and smiles slightly before walking off stage. Jack follows behind her.

Act 1
Scene III: *Granddad*

Sanford Care Home. Granddad's room. Granddad sits, hunched over, in his armchair which is positioned to the right-hand side of the stage. There is a bed on the other side of the room, and the only other furniture is a small table with a record player, three records, some rosary beads, an old-fashioned telephone and a black and white photograph of Granddad's late wife on it, in the centre of the stage. A clock is projected on the back wall, its hands completely still. Granddad is a quiet, lonely soul whose single moment of happiness each day is when his Granddaughter, Cara, comes to visit. He sits alone for a few moments before we hear Cara calling out to him from off-stage.

Cara   Granddad? Granddad? It's Cara!

Cara walks onto the stage and meets his gaze as he looks up expectantly from his chair. His face lights up. The hands on the clock behind him begin moving, faster than is realistic, to indicate how Granddad's world comes alive and animated with the arrival of Cara.

Cara   Hi Granddad!

Granddad Hiya love!

She sets her keys down on the table, puts her bag on the floor and goes over to Granddad in his chair. She gives him the warmest hug. Granddad is her person, the one who is always there, the one who gets her without even having to say a word. Both she and he relish this time together.

Cara   I'm so sorry I'm late… I got caught up at school… homework and that, you know what it's like. It's never ending!

Granddad chuckles and nods sympathetically but winces as he does so. We, of course, know that Cara is lying and she was actually 'caught up' with Maya and Jack but she doesn't let this on. Cara starts to busy herself in Grandad's room – putting keys down, picking things up off the floor, folding clothes, making the bed etc.

Cara *[attempting to change the subject]* Gosh, it's freezing in here! Have they fixed the heating yet?

Granddad *[laughing]* There's more chance of hell freezing over than them ever doing anything about that infernal boiler. Though I could've sworn I'd seen the Devil ice-skating past the other day so, you never know, we might be in luck next week!

Cara *Granddad!*

She smiles and walks over to the side of the stage and produces a blanket which she unfolds and puts over Grandad's legs. He winces slightly, trying to mask his pain from Cara.

Cara   Well, we can't have you getting a chill between now and next week then, can we? *[covering his feet with the blanket]*

Granddad   *[chuckles]* You worry too much *[dramatically with a smirk]* All of us have got at least one foot in the grave in here Cara. I'll be shaking hands with Elvis soon. If not today then tomorrow, next week if I don't talk back to the nurses!

Cara   [disapprovingly] The nurses are lovely!

Granddad [chuckles]

Granddad You're right. It's the doctors you've got to watch out for – the ones in this place are a thoroughly untrustworthy bunch. I'm telling you Cara; I'll catch my death in here soon.

Cara   [chuckling] Not while I'm around, you won't.

And don't say things like that

Granddad You know I'm only joking

Cara   [laughing] Well you're not funny

They both chuckle

Cara   Anyway, one of the nurses said that you'd already eaten - shepherd's pie, right? I can't believe I missed dinner. They always let me have the leftovers because, I mean, I'm here all the time - I practically live here at this point. The shepherd's pie is the best as well, although it doesn't even come close to Nana's, does it? Gosh, her cooking was famous all over Sandford - it was like her signature. She'd cook something for everything and anything and people would ask her to as well. Christening? Marie will cook. Birthday? Marie will cook. Anniversary? Marie again. Even funerals. And people loved her for it. Ah do you remember, whenever we came round- you'd answer the door she'd always be in the kitchen, singing along to Cliff Richard or John Denver and icing a Victoria sponge. And if we got there early enough she'd let me lick the cake batter off the spoon and...

She trails off. Granddad has gone quiet. His eyes are tightly shut, his face crumpled in pain. Something is wrong. She kneels down in front of him and puts her hands on his.

Cara   [confused] Granddad? What is it? Was it Nana, did I upset you? I'm so sorry...I... [pause, the penny drops] You're in pain aren't you? How long have you... Oh Grandad you must say something. Here...

She pulls out a small box of painkillers from behind the table and passes Granddad a pill along with his cup of tea which he takes without argument.

Cara   Alright, that's better. Now, we can just sit and be for a while. We can wait for that to kick in. It won't hurt for much longer.

But you've got to promise to tell me next time - *you are not a burden! You know me, once I get talking with you, I never stop! Go on, why don't you tell me one of your stories - take your mind off it? I've always loved them.*

Granddad   Okay, Did I ever tell you the story that the old woman back in the village told me?

Cara   No Granddad I don't think you did…

Granddad   Well I was an evacuee you know… back in the second world war. Lost both my parents. First my Dad went off to fight and then my Mum sent me out to the countryside to be safe from the bombs. That's how I ended up out here. The East End was no place for kids in the war. I'd never even seen a cow. I don't remember my Dad - he got killed in North Africa. That left just me and Mum - but I'd already been evacuated by then and she didn't tell me he was gone. Then Mum got bombed out. She didn't survive it. So I was left out here with nobody. The people who took me in as an evacuee were kind and they kept me - a bit like a stray. They brought me up. I was lucky really. It could have been much worse. I wouldn't have had nobody.

Cara   That's awful Granddad, no one ever told me about that

Granddad   Not so much to tell is there really? I tell you what though, around the end of the war, I was only about twelve - younger than you are now - an old lady in the village did tell me a story and I never forgot it.

Cara   What was that Granddad?

Granddad   She remembered something that happened in the first war you see… a girl in her village. People forget that in the first war they had rationing too – it came later but they had rationing alright. A lot of people went hungry. Hard times. Ordinary things. Bread. Meat. Milk. We take it for granted now love. It was bad during the second war too. I was very skinny. Not like I'm skinny now. I'm skinny now because I'm old. Anyway – where there's rationing there's a black market. People want things you see. So I'm told this lad was knocking around the village and he was a likely lad that thought he could make a bob or two. He was stealing chickens and selling eggs, meat - that type of thing… poaching. Anyway, this old woman told me that this lad caught the eye of every girl going because he seemed a bit fancy, he had some resources, and he could show them a bit of money. "An empty can rattles the loudest" - that's what she told me. She warned me. Anyway, this old lady said that one of the pretty girls in the village fell hook line and sinker for this toerag and they had a thing going. Until one day the girl got a warning of her own. She bumped into a gypsy see - who lived on the edge of the village. The woman told me that the Gypsy lady used to read palms and tea leaves and she was a bit spooky. Everyone left her to her own self. But this one day the girl stopped that Gypsy lady in her tracks - couldn't walk past her - "I don't see good things for you" this Gypsy lady said, pointing a boney finger.

Cara   Now Granddad…

Granddad   No, this Gypsy lady said to the pretty girl "You're up to no good with a boy from the village - that crooked lad will lead you

55

astray – crooked lads don't walk straight paths"

Cara   Probably very wise Granddad, I think those meds have kicked in now [to herself] ...*probably a little too much*

Granddad   No you see there's more… she said "You mark these words because I can see it, the boy you love will die in your arms and the church bells will ring out". The pretty girl paid it no mind and told the Gypsy lady she was bitter. Anyway – sure enough though that pretty girl was the talk of the village because a

month later she was out with
that lad and they were poaching.
Only the farmer saw them running
and he took a shot at them with
his gun. *You could do that then.*
A farmer took a shot at me once
and I tell you this I got down
out that apple tree fast. Where
was I? Oh yes. Now the shot hit
the lad and he went to the floor
and that girl held on to him.
Apparently, he didn't make it –
he passed away right there – and
sure enough the church bells
rang. *Just like that little old
gypsy woman warned that pretty
girl*. That's what I was told by
that woman. Still waters run
deep Cara. Find yourself a boy

isn't all on show. They'll all be competing for your attention soon you know. I won't always be around.

Cara   [she gets up and pulls Granddad's blanket up to his chest] Not if I have anything to do with it. Come on Granddad, I think I prefer the fairy tales! And I'm not sure you're supposed to call people 'gypsies' any more… Now you could do with a rest… Telling old wives' stories. I don't know. How about some music?

Granddad nods gratefully. Cara walks over to the table and places a record on the turntable of the record player. A 1950s rock and roll classic begins to play

[Song 4: Granddad and Cara's Duet]

Cara starts dancing across the stage in an attempt to cheer her Granddad up. At some point in the song, Cara dances over to her Granddad's chair and freezes by it. As though in flashback, Granddad gets up and dances. A woman, his late wife in younger form, glides onto the stage and dances with him. For just a moment, Granddad is freed from his age and decrepitude by the music. He attempts to kiss his wife on the cheek, but as the song ends, she is spirited away and Granddad goes to sit back in his chair. Cara unfreezes and continues dancing, her movements indicating a seated Granddad as her dance partner even though he cannot physically dance with her. She directs everything towards him in this beautiful moment of closeness and vulnerability, holding onto his hands as she sways from side to side and turning to mouth heartfelt lyrics to him as she moves. Granddad closes his eyes and falls asleep, completely content, as the song draws to a close. In the silence she holds onto his hand and kisses him on the cheek.

Cara   I promise you, I'm never going to leave you, Granddad. You'll never be on your own.

Act 1
Scene IV: *Cara's Bedroom*

The stage is split in half with a wall stretching across it from front to back. The left-hand side is empty for the moment, but the right-hand side has a bed placed in the middle of it (Cara's bedroom). Aside from the bed, Cara's bedroom is otherwise bare. It is a scene of loneliness and isolation. Cara walks into the room, still in her school uniform, and slings her bag onto the floor. She falls back onto her bed and lies there, completely still for a moment. She sighs and puts her hands on her face before throwing them out to the side. She then sits up, crosses her legs and pulls out her phone. A projection of her phone screen appears above the stage. We see her scrolling through her apps before finding 'contacts' where she then clicks on 'Mum'. The dial tone sounds loudly for what feels like an age. Then to voicemail.

Voicemail [Cara's Mum's voice]   Hello, you've reached the voicemail for Professor Walker, I'm not available at the moment. You can contact my personal assistant by re-dialling to extension 38●. Please don't leave a message here because I don't respond to voicemail – but do send me an email for anything more urgent. Thank you. *[phone gives a loud beep]*

Cara   Hi Mum, I know you check these… sorry – it's only me. I've probably called at a bad time. You're busy. Maybe it's bad reception or something – I don't know – anyway I just wanted to call you to see how you are and how things are going at work? I hope the jet lag isn't too bad – or not as bad as last time anyway. Actually, I think you get the jet lag coming back from there? Anyway – sorry – erm. I went to see Granddad today and he's kind of the same – but they've upped his medication a bit. Apparently, he's been in some pain – actually quite a lot but you know that he doesn't really tell. I can see it though. *[Pause]* I think the extra meds are helping - he seemed a bit better… *[pause]* Erm I've got a school concert happening on Friday and I wondered if you might be back in time and if you could make it? I mean - no problem if not - it's fine either way…

Voicemail [interrupting Cara] This voicemail box is now full. Please try again later.

Cara is cut off in the middle of her message. She lies down across her bed in frustration and drops her phone on the bed next to herself.

Cara   I mean it's fine either way. Totally. I know that work comes first right. And wherever you and whatever it is that you're doing has to happen so… you know… it's not like I actually expect you to be there with the other parents, because why would we do that right? I'll call Dad and see if he's too busy as well. Cheers.

She stares at the wall. She shouts the word "Daaaad" just in case – by some miracle – they happen to be in the same building at the same time. There's no answer. He's still at work too. She flicks through her numbers to 'Dad' and presses the green dial button. It rings.

Dad   Hiya love – what's wrong?

Cara   Nothing – I just wondered if you'd be home for dinner?

Dad   Oh yeah – sorry love – what time is it?

Cara   Oh, it's like five or something…

Dad   Wow… look I'll probably get a pizza– I'm rushed off my feet. You ok?

Cara   Yeah – I mean poor you… look I could have something ready that you can reheat? You don't

	get paid enough for all those hours Dad
Dad	I know right – I seriously do not. I'm sorry love.
Cara	It's not your fault – I'll make double and you can reheat it when you get in
Dad	You're my Angel Princess.
Cara	Well I can be one or the other Dad I don't think Angel-Princesses are actually a thing

Dad   *[chuckles]* You're probably right - look I gotta go. Did you hear from your Mother?

Cara   Professor Walker cannot answer at the moment… AND that bloody machine cut me off again.

Dad   Hey tell me about that right. I have some of my best conversations with that machine. Before it cuts me off. *[speaks to someone in his office]* Yeah - I got that - ok… Baby I gotta go love you!

Cara   Love…

Dad hangs up.

Cara   …you too

Cara feels utterly dejected and her isolation is bearing down on her. This is a regular experience - but it has been getting increasingly common the older she gets. She presses down her sense of rejection and turns her attention instead to social media - scrolling through her messages. There are seven missed calls from Jack and one voicemail. She looks around.

A Devil and an Angel silently enter her room from different directions. They are unsettling and mysterious characters. Both are invisible to Cara and all other characters on stage (besides each other) who take no notice of their appearance or dialogue. Their presence is purely for the viewer's benefit and as a result, they are only visible to the audience.

Cara   Voicemail? I don't get voicemail - I don't even know how to call voicemail. I mean I know how to leave one obviously but...what the hell?

The Devil   [whispers] Google it

Cara   Wait - I'll Google it -

Cara searches the internet to find out how to receive a voicemail message - she finds that she has to dial 197 on her phone.

Angel   [whispers] 1 9 6, ONE NINE SIX!

Cara   Who even leaves voicemail? *Apart from me*. Obviously. What was it – wait – 197 or 196?

We see her type '1 9 7' into her keypad. The Devil smirks at the Angel as if to say "*nice try*"

Voicemail   Welcome to voicemail. You have one new message. To play the message press 1. To delete the message press 2. To hear these options again press 3

Angel   [*whispers*] 2 it's 2. Press 2.

Cara   Was it 1 or 2? Was it 1 or 2??! What do I do now?! I think it

                        was 2 - it was 2... it was. *[Cara
                        presses 2]*

Voicemail   You have deleted... 1 new message

Now the Angel smirks at the Devil and shows him the middle finger and nods like "Yeah I did".

Cara   WHAT!!?

For a very long and frozen moment Cara, The Angel and The Devil stare collectively at her handset. The tension is real.

Cara   *You actually deleted that message? From Jack? Are you an actual idiot? Oh my days.*

Voicemail   To recover this message press 1, to permanently delete this message press 2

The Angel   *[Whispers] two!!*

The Devil   *Shut up you Angel! ONE ONE ONE!*

The Angel   *[whispers] two!*

Cara   TWO, TWO – *definitely* TWO

Voicemail   This message will be *permanently* deleted – are you sure? Press 1 to confirm or 2 to cancel and return to the menu

The Devil death stares at The Angel

Cara   WHAT IS GOING ON?! ACTUALLY??

                    Ughhh Cara, are you stupid?!!!

Cara guides her finger to the 1 button with her other hand – the Angel is nodding furiously; the Devil is shaking his head… but at the last minute Cara stops – both Angel and Devil are frozen looking at her like "What now?!"

The Devil   I'm a prince of the underworld and I ain't never seen anything like this. This is some stupid shit going on right here. I mean what 15-year-old doesn't know how to use a bloody phone?

Cara   WAIT! If I confirm that – that means 'do delete it', and… I want 'don't delete it' – right? *[blows air out hard]* I think I want 2. Please be 2.

The Devil   Well done genius.

Cara presses the number 2 with great deliberation.

The Devil   Right, we're back in the game!

Voicemail   Welcome to voicemail. You have one new message. To play the message press 1 now, to delete the message press 2. To hear these options again, press 3.

Cara	Oh my God, it's still there! It's still there! Ok I get why Mum hates voicemail now. *[Cara presses 1 - carefully]* Does this happen every time you get a voicemail? Jesus…

The Devil settles back smugly and raises a middle finger to The Angel and mouths "Yeah bitch". The Angel rolls her eyes and shakes her head.

Voicemail (Jack's voice)	Hi Cara, it's me Jack - why aren't you picking up? Seriously! There's something about you Cara. You're not like any other girl I've ever met. I can't work you out… you don't give anything away… you're

mysterious to me, you're beautiful, you're deep, you make me feel like I'm drunk, or high or something. How have you even done this to me? *[long pause]* You said that you need me to be serious for you, serious about you… I just need you to know that…

Voicemail   The message length is full. To call back press 1, to delete this message press 2, to return to the main menu press 3. You have no saved messages.

The Angel now looks smug and returns two fingers in the direction of the Devil and mouths "SUCK ON THAT BIG BOY". The Devil looks suitably unimpressed.

CARA	WHAAAAT?! YOU JUST NEED ME TO KNOW WHAT? WHAT DO YOU NEED ME TO KNOW JACK?? What did he *even* say: "I just want you to know that you're not worth the effort"?

"I just want you to know that I'm gay and your masculine features helped me to sort out my conflicted journey into my sexual identity?"

Is he serious? Is he even… *[pause]* actually… *[pause]* serious?

What should I do now?

Cara buries her head under her pillow and screams into her mattress.

The Devil   Nice one. Nice one. You know for an Angel you really know how to upset children don't you.

The Angel   *[Looks on furious]* Don't you play that with me you ought to get the hell out of here

The Devil   The *hell* I will

[Song 5: Cara's Conflict]

Music begins to play - it's a song that reflects Cara's inner turmoil. Cara knows that Jack is bad news and he'll bring her nothing but trouble - but she wants him so badly. She wants the excitement, the drama, the attention, the jealousy… she needs to escape the terrible boredom of the life

that she has. As Cara begins to sing, the Devil and the Angel fight over her - pulling her by the arms both left and right, turning her around and confusing her. The song reflects both the sensible notions that she could find a sweet boy with good manners and prospects, but also the dark, intoxicating brand of excitement that Jack appears to offer. The alternative verses, choruses and conflicting and contradictory lines express all the confusion and naivety inside Cara's head.

As this continues, Jack and his friends enter and occupy the other side of the stage and mime their conversations and jokes…

Even though they are actually miles apart, Jack and Cara turn to face each other through the wall separating them and she feels as if she has been zapped with forked lightening.

The Devil quietly slips Cara's phone into her palm.

Cara sends a message to Jack. Celebrating his success, the Devil slips away, donning a hoodie to go and stand now with Jack and his friends. The Angel sits, defeated. Head in hands.

Jack and his friends come to life as the text message arrives instantly to start Act 1 Scene 5.

Act 1

Scene V: *Toxic Masculinity*

Jack receives a message from Cara and he is bragging with his mates outside the local shop (Jon, Tom and the Devil who is now dressed in the same style as the boys). The Devil nods, laughing along. They're drinking out of open cans and they're smoking.

Jack   Shut up you tart! Liverpool?! You haven't even been to Liverpool! You don't even know where it is mate. Win the league? Mate I'll have a pony on it with you – it's Man City this year…

Jon   City buy everything mate – I haven't been to Liverpool? Point to Manchester on a map then! At least my dad's *from* Liverpool – you don't even know where your Dad's from mate

Tom   Burn!

Jack   You *think* you know where your dad's from, but you don't know where your Mum's *been*

Tom   Oooooh damn!

A mobile phone alert sounds – Cara's message arrives on Jack's phone…

Jack   Hey - hey - look at this [face lighting up] You know what this means… shows the message to Tom first

Jon   Let me see, let me see!

Jack   Oi dick head!

Jon   No come on… [they play wrestle]

Jack   I told you she wanted it… she so wants it

Tom   What does it say?

Jack   It says [reading so they can't see the screen] "I really want you now, you are so hot come and give it to me"

[on the back of the stage the actual words are projected from Cara "I've been thinking about u – are u serious?"]

Jon   Shut up you div she didn't

Tom   Is that what it says? Shiiiit

Jon   Course it doesn't say that you dickhead

Tom   What does it say?

Jack   Shut up, shut up, I'm replying

Jon   What a liar

Jack   [Speaking out words] "I... AM... GOING... TO... GIVE... IT... TO... YOU... YOU... DIRTY... COW"

[on the back of the stage "Yeah x I'm serious x You're special Princess x"]

Tom   You didn't send that? *You mad man!*

Jack   Watch and learn boys – treat 'em mean...

Tom   Keep 'em keen?

Jack   *Er... no* – just treat em mean... ?

Mobile alert sounds again... Cara's reply reads: 'I wondered if we could meet up?'

Jack   She's saying what she's going to do to me… OH MY GOD LADS this one is filthy – I'm not even letting you read this, you'll go blind.

Tom   Don't even be like that

Jon   He's messing you around – it's not even her – it's some number he put in his phone under her name. It's an overweight 50-year-old paedophile that's been grooming him for like two weeks. What a gay boy.

Jack   Mate you're just pissed off cause you owe me money over this

Jon   What – I bet you that you couldn't shag that plain bitch out of science – not get a text off her. Anyone can slide into the DMs of a desperate ugly cow. If it wasn't for desperate ugly cows you'd still be a virgin and your Dad wouldn't have had your mum

Tom   *Oh damn*

Jack It's a good job that you're my boy or I would have messed you up for that [smiling and laughing, preoccupied texting back: 'We can go wherever you want to Princess']

I'm telling her how to fondle my balls

Jon   I hope she's got hands like a man cause that's how you like your balls fondled at the gay bar

Jack You better have my money ready because she's salivating mate.

Jon   You better get evidence or I'm not gonna pay mate. I mean *video*.

Jack I'll get video, I'll get video of me leaving and I'll get video of me never going back either… ha ha

Tom   You're a legend. No no, mate, mate – you have to go back and break up with her after and then get a photo of her desperate face crying with her tits out and we'll put it on the notice board at school

Jon   OH, HELL YEAH and we'll put it up just before we hit a fire alarm AND EVERYONE WILL WALK PAST IT

Tom   I'll print out a load and leave them in the area where everyone goes on the fire alarm - just scatter them over the field - OH IT WILL BE BRUTAL MATE

Jon   Damn it's worth a tenner. I don't mind paying up on that, I'm not gonna lie.

Cara's message alert sounds:

[You gotta be straight with me – are you genuine because I'm not one of those girls and I'm worried you're just gonna hurt me?]

Jon   Oh she's begging you bro… I'm not gonna lie – proud of you [they have a unique fist bump]

Jack dances a little like there is music playing.

He texts Cara back: 'Don't worry. I wouldn't ever hurt an Angel. I promise you. We can just take things really slow and get to know each other. I just want to be your friend first.'

Jack   I'm telling Cara I don't wear condoms – screw it – let's get that out of the way. That shit is on her.

Jon   Literally.

Tom   That's her problem bro.

The Devil nudges one of the boys and they notice that Aiden has been hovering in the doorway a little while. They don't know how long or what he has heard. In reality he hasn't heard the nasty scheme they've got planned -

Jack   What the fuck is this? Can I help you bro? Did they have your tampons yeah? The brand you like?

Aiden   Hi Mate…

Jack   Right [looks at Jon and shakes his head]

Jon   Aiden you need to shave your legs for your boyfriend yeah – don't forget to get some of those pink razors and shit… do you need to go back in yeah?

Tom   Laughing

Jack   [Nods – gives Tom a handshake to say 'good one']

Aiden   [Smiles a wry smile to say 'hot line' or 'good one' as he walks awkwardly by] Fair – that's a good line though…

They watch Aiden walk away – allow him to get all the way to the other side of the stage…

Jack   Aiden Mate [friendly tone] – Mate! Mate! I've got something for you

Aiden   [walks back a long way from where he was] Yeah?

Jack   [produces his middle finger from his pocket] One of those mate

Jon & Tom   Burst out laughing

Act 2

Act 2

Scene I: *The Party*

Party Prelude

The following is displayed on a big screen at the front of the stage (shown in portrait to simulate a huge phone screen) the messages will 'arrive' and be 'exchanged' as if the characters are all arranging a social event with Jack:

Big Man Jack	Hey guys party at mine. Friday. 10PM
Moaner	YH alright
Juicy Lucy	Weed?
Big Man Jack	Obvs
Jon	Im in
Big Man Jack	Someone bring drinks tho

Tommy	No Im broke
Big Man Jack	Then dont come
Tommy	Prick
Jon	Whos gonna b there?
Big Man Jack	Idk evil one
Big Man Jack	*everyone
Big Man Jack	Ducking autocorrect
Big Man Jack	Ffs
Tommy	Bro ru like 90 lol lern to type
Big Man Jack	Shut up
Moaner	Hey jack i heard you and cara r a thing wtf?
Juicy Lucy	Wait wat?
Big Man Jack	Yh so?
Juicy Lucy	Stfu
Moaner	Omg eww ur not bringing her tho right?

Big Man Jack	Yh i am wot r u gonna do
Moaner	Ffs do you have to?
Juicy Lucy	Serious jack pls dont
Moaner	We dont like her we got beef
Dani the Slag	Whats happening someone explain
Juicy Lucy	No
Dani the Slag	I cba to read all teh monsters
Dani the Slag	*messages
Big Man Jack	Pahah Tom not just me mate
Moaner	Ugh fine Party Fri 10Pm Bring drink
Dani the Slag	K
Moaner	Cara's coming
Dani the Slag	OML r u for real?
Moaner	No tho

Big Man Jack	My party deal with
Moaner	Ur not even with her coz you like her ur just using her
Big Man Jack	Yh and?
Tommy	And ur problem?
Big Man Jack	Exactly
Jon	Oi Jack tenner if u can get that stiff high
Big Man Jack	Ur on
Tommy	Ur a mad man Jack never happen

As the screen is removed from the stage we are taken to the outside of Jack's house. The stage curtains remain shut. Cara enters from the back of the theatre, from behind the audience, and begins to walk down the aisle towards the stage. She is dressed as if she is going out: sequined dress, curled *hair, red lipstick, and heels. The stage curtains are closed but we can hear the thumping of a heavy rap beat and muffled chatter from behind them. As Cara walks towards the stage, Jack appears from the gap in between the curtains on his phone. He sees Cara and puts it in his back pocket.*

Jack   Hey you

Cara   Hey

Jack   I'm so glad you came to this

Cara   I don't even know what 'this' is – like what am I even doing here

Jack   You'll see

Cara   I got ready just like you said: something nice, something pretty but I don't know Jack, I feel like it's too much [gesturing to her outfit] is it too much [she twirls]? It's too much isn't it? Are they all wearing hoodies? Oh my God they're all wearing hoodies in there aren't they?

Jack   It's fine… you look… fiiiine [devouring her with his eyes – she looks every bit as good as he hoped that she would – and more] Come on.

Cara looks unsure, she's hesitant, but Jack takes her by the hand and leads her up towards the curtains. He opens them slightly, creating a small gap which he and

Cara peer through. She feels like Cinderella.

Jack   What do you think? Pretty cool, right? You said you'd never been to a party, a proper one, so I did this all for you.

Cara   No way! I mean it looks awesome but I don't know I thought it was just going to be you and me this evening. Are you sure these people want me here? *I know these guys don't like me* [she gestures discreetly to a group hidden behind the curtains which is later revealed to be Maya and her clique]

Jack   [Looks Cara up and down] They'll like you now

Cara   What's that supposed to mean?

Jack   Now you're less… well… you know what I mean. *Plus, you're mine*

Cara looks unconvinced

Jack   Cara, lighten up! This is your party! *You've got this.* There's music, drinks, everyone's here – oh, and I got you *this*…

Jack produces a small silver box with a luxurious turquoise bow on it

Cara   What is *this*?

Jack   Open it! Go on… I want to see your face…

Cara opens the bow slowly and flips open the box to reveal a locket – it's silver, ornate, expensive looking and a little bit ostentatious. Cara has never been presented with such a thing. It is incredibly unexpected. She struggles to find words and this absolutely not what she expected from Jack.

Cara   Oh my God… it's beautiful… how? Where? What even is this? This must have cost a fortune!

A 'party goer' (the Devil) seems to bump into Jack – almost spoiling the moment – but whispers in Jack's ear and then staggers away pointing back at them and giving a 'thumbs up' gesture…

Jack   Oh… [Lies] Well we don't have much in our family but that got passed to me and I was told to only give it to a girl that I was really, really serious about… and I just kinda wanted you to know that you're not like other girls.

Cara   Jack you didn't need to do this…

Jack   I wanted to do this Cara. And besides… I'm doing really well for myself. I have money coming in, I have solid contacts and a proper business going. I could buy you

>   whatever you want: shoes, dresses, make-up – literally anything…

Cara turns back around and smiles at Jack

Cara   I like other things besides clothes and concealer Jack. I'm not that shallow.

Jack   Whatever! Other things then! What matters is that I'm making a killing now

He smiles back and then disappears behind the curtain through the gap, leaving CARA alone on the front of the stage.

Cara   That's what worries me

She hesitates for a moment before entering the party through the curtains, leaving an empty stage. The curtains open, revealing a chaotic, hedonistic party atmosphere: flashing multicoloured lights, loud music, people dancing and smoking. There are spilled drinks and drunken shouting. The Devil is playing one of his games: He has spiked a drink and he is watching to see who will end up drinking from it. We watch him slip a powder into a clear glass (for the awareness of the audience, the liquid changes to a vibrant, garish green) The drink is passed around amongst the partygoers like a curious game of Russian roulette- but they remain oblivious. The rest of the drinks at the party are either coloured clear (vodka) or black (coke) to further highlight the presence of the contaminated drink. To begin, with the Devil puts the contaminated cup straight into the hands of Dani who is about to take a sip:

Dani: *[Raises the glass to her mouth but at the last moment sees Maya]* Oh hey Maya!! *[She passes the glass off to Lucy who is standing nearby]*

Lucy now has two glasses and looks at the glass Dani has just given her and puts it down on the table at the front of the stage.

The Angel is sat slightly separated from the main group of dancers and drinkers, silently sipping from a bottle – as if defeated. Cara stands awkwardly at the side of the room: she wants to be there but doesn't at the same time. The people at the party make her feel profoundly uncomfortable. Aiden appears from within the commotion and spots her. Cara seems relieved.

Aiden   Cara! Hi! I didn't expect to see you here [Aiden picks up *the drink* from the table] Would you like a drink?

Cara   Oh no - not for me - not really my thing but thanks. Anyway - I didn't think that this was your scene? Or your kind of people?

Aiden   *[hands the drink to Maya as she walks past- Maya takes it, scowling, but is too cool to 'accept' a drink from Aiden and puts it down elsewhere in the room without drinking from it]* They're not really but Olly asked if I'd go with, and I couldn't really say no. He saw through all of my excuses. He's here for the girls though. I'm here to carry him home once he's too pissed to walk. What about you?

Cara   Well, me and Jack… we're… kind of a thing…

Aiden No kidding? [trying not to look too emotionally invested in this news, but in reality – he's crushed]

Cara   Yeah – it's been about two weeks…

Aiden And he's already buying you necklaces… [trying to disguise his envy and bitterness]

Cara   What? [looking down towards the locket in a slightly shocked way] How could you know it was from him, he only just gave it to me?

Aiden   [fighting the urge to say "He uses drug money to buy a locket for every girl he goes out with"] Cause it's totally not your usual style – I mean you'd never normally wear that sort of thing. I mean. You could do – if you want to – you look lovely.

Cara   *Damn*. I mean, you're right, but…

Aiden   [nervous and feeling conspicuous] You forget that I've known you, like, since, forever.

Cara   True! [nervous laugh]

Aiden   Sorry - I didn't mean to sound creepy.

Cara   No - I'm just not used to anyone noticing me.

Aiden   You can be anything you want to be Cara.

Jack   Cara! Hey Cara!

Jack is seated amongst a cluster of his friends including Tom, Maya and Jon, beer in one hand and a large ostentatious joint in the other. Two girls are draped on his shoulders. Cara immediately gets up and moves towards Jack, leaving Aiden without saying good-bye

Aiden   Bye Cara... [she doesn't hear this or respond due to the loud music and the commotion of the party – Aiden feels ghosted]

Jack   Come and sit with me gorgeous. Do you want a drink babe?

Cara   Nah – I'm good thanks [nervous smile]

Jack   Oh go on – don't be square, everyone likes a drink…

Jack picks up a glass from the table – whether he knows it or not, it is the contaminated drink which has made its way round to Jack's table – he offers it to Cara. Holding the glass nervously, contemplating downing the whole thing in one hit, Cara lifts it towards her mouth before pausing for a moment. A tray is dropped in the background and drinks clatter to the floor. As everyone turns around and laughs, Cara puts the glass back on the table

Cara   Actually, I'm good thanks Babe

Tom   Ooh Jack, she'll keep you in line mate – bit stiff that one

Maya Aww poor Cara, she's definitely one of those uptight ones who doesn't swear or smoke [she whispers into Jack's ear] and I bet she won't shag you either

Jon   Aw she probably hasn't popped her cherry yet… don't worry baby, you'll love it once you get the first time out of the way… [he laughs crudely]

Maya Pahaha did you mean to pick out the only virgin in the school jack? There are girls arriving in Year 7 that have already done what she won't do…

Jack   [laughing] Piss off you lot. {turns to Cara more softly] Just have a drink Cara – *it won't kill you* [sarcastically and turning towards Maya] you might even have some fun…

Jack passes Cara a fresh drink. It is not contaminated. She takes it and sips at it reluctantly. Her consent has been broken. It doesn't really matter if she wants to drink or not.

The music changes into an upbeat tempo. The group make their way to the centre of the stage where people are dancing. Jack gets up close to Cara, they are intimately inside each other's personal space. He reaches the necklace, opens the locket and produces a single tablet from inside it. He brings the tablet up to Cara's lips – which

121

are closed - and in a slow movement, looking her in the eyes he goes to kiss her. As she closes her eyes and opens her mouth, he doesn't kiss her, instead he pops the pill into her mouth. Cara's eyes widen as if to communicate that this is not what she wanted she shakes her head slightly, but she is shushed by Jack who places a finger on her lips

Jack   I know you're struggling here. This will make it easier for you. I got it for you. I just want you to have a good time. I'll never hurt you…

Cara closes her eyes and swallows. She takes a long drink from her glass.

Tom   Go on Jack mate - you're the only person I know who can rap…

Jon   Yeah go on mate, you got bars mate!

The girls chorus their encouragement with "Go on Jack!"

Jack   [Feigning disinclination] Naaa

Maya   Jack! Jack! Jack! Jack!

This is exactly what Jack wanted and as the chant grows louder and more people join in. Clapping and stamping starts. Jack smiles wryly…

Jack   Ok - I'll do it for Cara…

[Song 6: Jack's party rap]

Jack kicks the bottles and the garbage off the table, before standing on his little podium.

Whilst Jack is rapping people cheer and dance and the Devil continues his 'patrol' of the party. Cara is now well on her way - taking rounds of shots and laughing wildly. She is messy and disinhibited through drink and drugs. She finally feels liberated and popular in a way that she never has been - and never realised that she wanted to feel. She is happy.

The Angel and Aiden sit in the corner.

When Jack finishes his rap, Cara finds herself sitting with several girls: Maya's crew. Everyone is very intoxicated.

Maya [shouting over the music] You know Cara, you're actually kind of cool. Once you loosen up.

Cara [overconfident and disinhibited] You know it! Whoooo!

Lucy [laughing] Yeah, you should let your hair down with us more often girl - you're kinda gorgeous…

Dani Yeah I'm jealous - *let's be honest* - we'd all like a piece of Jack!

Maya And I know what piece I want bitches! Ha ha ha!

Dani   You must have sent some seriously good pics to have hooked him, if you know what I mean. *Is that how you got him to say yes?*

Cara   Well actually… I'm not gonna lie… [drunken pause]

The Devil floats by with the contaminated drink and puts it in Dani's hand. She accepts it gratefully and takes a sip. This action must be done as obviously and clearly as possible in order to make the audience aware that Dani has drunk the contaminated liquid.

Lucy   What *did* you do Cara? Did you… [makes an obscene hand gesture that simulates male masturbation]

Cara *No! I mean, not yet!* [bursts out laughing and covers her face with her hands – she is very messy and uncoordinated]

Maya Well what then? Come on, what's the secret?

Cara …he just asked me, and at first I thought he was taking the piss so I just ignored him. He just kept asking. So eventually I said ok.

Maya [stunned for a moment by this apparent hardnosed and inadvertently genius tactic] I can't believe it. *You* played it cool?

Cara   I didn't 'play it' anything
       [laughing]

Jack joins the group and the intimate 'girls room' atmosphere changes again as all the girls want to impress Jack, look good in front of him, and flirt with him – even with Cara right there. There is an absolutely ironic 'try hard', 'pick me' quality about them. Cara is too wasted to notice.

Jack   [to Cara] Hey Babe…

Jack is so far gone that he's now slurring his words.

Jack   Has anyone ever told you that you're totally fucking fit?

Cara   I've told you before babe… [teasing in front of the other girls] *you'll be the first.*

Cara and Jack lock eyes and although the whole party is around them – and just about every girl is watching this unfold – Cara feels like she is only seen by Jack. She looks into his eyes and feels completely absorbed by him. She is falling. Jack returns this look, and it is heated with adolescent sexual urgency – if he thought he could get away with it, he would jump her right there

Dani   [Jealously] Eew get a room

Jack   Jealous?

Dani   Not of you, man-whore [she jokingly winds up her middle finger at him and pokes out her tongue]. I'm getting another drink…

Dani leaves her phone and clutch bag with Maya and walks unsteadily to the centre of the stage. She is clearly very drunk - but there is something hitting much harder and much faster now. She is disoriented and her balance is going. She looks around in distress with wide eyes.

The music dies down to a stop.

The strobe light and party lights continue. People are still dancing - but out of time and with no beat or sense.

[A high pitch drone - like a ringing in the ears is played through the theatre.]

Dani strains her eyes to try to focus. She knocks over a table of glasses. Someone mouths "What the fuck?" She clumsily grabs at a drinks bottle and tries to remove the cap. She misses with the 'bottle opener' – which is actually a car key.

The Angel moves in quickly and helps Dani down to the floor as she passes out. She looks around desperately and waves frantically in front of Dani's face. Nobody responds or pays any attention. As Dani gets more comatose, she can actually see the Angel and shapes her hands to her face. Dani tried to kiss the Angel and says

Dani   You're so beautiful! Who even are you? I've never seen you before…

The Angel evades the kiss and looks only more worried. The living are not supposed to be able to see or hear her.

The Angel   What? You shouldn't be able to see...It's ok. Stay where you are. Just stay where you are. This is not your time. This is *not* your time.

Ignoring the apparent emergency, Jon moves in on Dani, sensing her vulnerability. He brings a blanket with him. Feigning concern, he sweeps the blanket over her.

Jon   It's ok baby – *I'll* look after you

Dani murmurs in response but cannot verbalise. Her body feels disconnected and unavailable to her

Jon   Oh you like that?

He puts his hands under the blanket and begins to explore her body while she has no ability to stop him, to object or offer any form of consent. The Angel watches on, bitterly viewing everything that Jon is doing and utterly helpless. As Jon continues, another friend wheels past and gives him a fist bump and a smile. Jon has a cruel grin on his face. Dani is conscious and breathing – but she has no freedom and no agency of her own at all… This continues as the lights lower for the end of the scene. The rest of the party continue oblivious.

Act 2

Scene II: *The Hangover*

The morning after the party. It's a mess. There are dirty cups and packets of half-eaten food spread across the floor, spilled drinks, chairs knocked over and people sprawled across each other in varying states of consciousness and undress.

Maya, Lucy and two other members of their gang are sitting, leaning against the table at the front of the stage. Cara is asleep on the floor beside them. The Angel is walking around with a black bin liner, tossing cups, cigarette ends and drug related paraphernalia into it whilst talking to the Devil who sits on top of the table that the girls are leaning against.

Angel   God, what a mess, they don't call you 'the tempter' for nothing do they?

Devil   What can I say? I'm the best at what I do. It has to be said though, most of them brought this upon themselves.

Angel   You really have no shame

Devil   Oh go on, polish your halo all you like but I didn't see you doing all that much to prevent whatever it is that you so strongly disapprove of. "Lead us not into temptation", my arse! You angels are always happy to watch but never happy to get your hands dirty!

The Angel takes offence and throws an empty bottle at the Devil's face, but he catches it with one hand and sticks his middle finger up at the Angel with the other. Whilst this is happening, Cara begins to stir. She sits up slowly and gathers her senses.

Cara   Oh my god, my head…

Maya   Ohhhh it lives!!

Lucy   Shhh Maya – my head is splitting. Go easy on her, it's probably her first time…

Maya   Oh yeah… first timer [nudges Lucy suggestively with a wink]. Wakey wakey Cara…

Cara   Urgh I feel like I'm dying. What the hell happened?

Maya   Cheap vodka…

Lucy   Weed and MDMA

Cara   *Where's Jack?*

Maya and Lucy together   [laughing in unison] And Jack!

Maya   Those things are a bad combination, and you can believe me… *I've had all of them!* I'm surprised that you're not still throwing up.

Cara   *Still?* What? Was I sick?

Lucy   Er yeah - just a bit - you really heaved.

Cara   Do you guys do this every weekend?

Maya   We can't always afford it - *but we try*

[Song 7: Acapella 'hangover' rap (reprise of Act 1 Acapella Rap)]

Maya and Lucy construct an impromptu rap - and usually this involves Dani - who is nowhere to be found. Cara is urged to take Dani's place. Initially this involves her having to sing or hum through a basic melody/harmony part (instructed by the girls) - but turns on Cara when she is asked to improvise a verse of rhyme and rap in front of them. It feels like an initiation into their group.

With the relief of her uncomfortable rap performance out of the way Cara apologises, exits the room, and vomits outside from sheer anxiety. She is feeling incredibly misplaced in this scene now that the drink and the drugs have worn off and she is not at all comfortable. She feels like an imposter.

Cara groans, returning to the room, as Dani appears, wrapped in a blanket, disoriented, and apparently looking for her clothes. Her mouth is stained with the same colour as the drug-cocktail. Her hair is a mess and she has love bites on her neck.

Maya	Oooh look at the state of this [takes photo on mobile]

Lucy	Where have you been?

Dani	I don't really remember…

Maya	*Not again*

Dani	I swear - I just woke up outside… but... I didn't think I went outside. How long was I out there? I wouldn't go outside without someone else…

[she looks increasingly worried and disoriented]

Lucy   Come on mate you were *seriously* pissed – you wouldn't have a clue

Dani   Genuinely – I just remember getting another drink and it went black – then I'm outside and my body aches… I'm covered in bruises…

Maya   It's just another hangover – another day in the life of Dani. It'll come back to you mate. I wonder who the lucky fella was this time. The real question is – *is he ok?*

Lucy   Such a lightweight. Get over it – this has happened to us all…

Dani   You're right… you're right… have you seen my top anywhere?

Cara   Guys, this doesn't feel right to me – don't you think this is worrying?

Maya   Chill out Cara – trust me this is not her first rodeo…

Jon and Tom enter. Dani goes to leave the stage.

Jon	Oi oi Dani – don't be shy – you weren't last night honey!

Dani	And you can fuck right off!

Jon	And I was just saying how much we enjoyed ourselves last night Dani. Hey come and feel this [he gestures towards his jumper] go on… feel that… you know what that feels like?

Dani	[touches the jumper] What?

Jon   It feels like boyfriend material right? Ha ha ha

Tom   Come on bro – who wants to boyfriend that?!

Dani is oblivious to what happened last night and she is still deeply confused but she plays along because she doesn't want to look like she wasn't in control of herself.

Dani   I'm sure I didn't enjoy anything with you mate

Jon   That's not what I remember

Tom   Come on now Dani… you're dangerous you are. One of these days you're gonna get one of us boys in trouble. You know how you get towards the end of the evening, you're always taking advantage. I'm not even joking you need to take more care and responsibility [laughing].

Dani   [mute stare]

Tom   [mutters to Jon] Tread carefully mate I don't think she has a clue.

Jon [Loudly] That's bad. I'm not gonna lie. I feel used. I'm not a piece of meat you know. I actually feel like I'm losing my self-respect. This is all so shallow. Urgh I feel so dirty.

Tom You're not a *big* piece of meat you mean.

Jon Funny guy. Didn't pick you though did she?

Dani looks on at Jon with a scowl, shakes her head and looks away with a feeling of humiliation that is very real.

Jack enters and immediately goes over to Cara. He sits down next to her.

Jack Hey Babe

Cara Hey... I don't think everything is ok with Dani… I think something happened to her last night and she's playing it off like it was nothing.

Jack You don't know what Dani is like. When you get to know Dani you'll find out that she loved every minute of it at the time. There isn't a boy here who hasn't…

Cara   Jack! I don't think she consented to anything - she was in a complete state

Jack   Dani doesn't know how to say no when she's sober mate. Forget it. She's a slag.

Cara   Don't call her that!

Jack   Why not? She's an absolute bike mate. Chill out.

Cara   Look… I just… [rubs her forehead]

Tom   I'm going back to bed - has anyone got any fags?

Jon   Shut up and buy your own

The two boys leave, holding each other up in hangover sympathy.

Jack   I'm going out for baccy - I'll be ten minutes - 'backie' in a bit Babe! Backie - get it?! *Damn I'm good...*

[Song 8: Dani's Song - Solo]

Dani takes the centre of the stage as everyone else fades into their hangover state. She sings a heartfelt song about feeling used, unvalued, and not knowing what has happened to her. The song encompasses her sense of low self-esteem and speaks of modest and honest aspirations that she dare not share with her friends because she is scared that they might laugh at her and reject her for being 'square'. She reveals that she is gay and that she has no interest in the boys but doesn't want to be unpopular and risk being rejected by the group.

Act 2

Scene III: *Aiden's Room*

We are transported to the tranquillity and peace of Aiden's bedroom. It is a tidy, well organised personal space of eclectic tastes and diverse influences and provides a stark visual contrast to Cara's empty bedroom. It demonstrates a person who has made choices about who they are based on the sampling of many things. Aiden is a lover of reading so there are books spilling over his shelf and onto the floor. He listens to music on vinyl and has a record collection. On the walls, instead of posters of naked women and girls, he has prints by artists like Mark Rothko and Yoko Ono. The only picture of a woman on his wall is young Ruth Bader Ginsberg, which serves as his inspiration. A healthy and well-tended plant is on his desk. He has a dog, 'Boomer', to whom he shows lots of affection. He is at his desk, but he isn't working. He is wrapped up in his thoughts. He occasionally shakes his head as if he is in a conversation with himself. Despite his apparently quite pensive state, the pervasive mood remains calm and peaceful. The Angel sits on the bed leafing through a book: listening. Aiden is clearly oblivious.

Aiden   How do you even? I mean… right? If I can't even say the words *here* there's no way that I can say it to her. It's just like every time I see her my heart just wants to stop dead and tell me that it quits. My mouth goes dry. I can't speak. My feet feel like concrete… *oh this is awful.*

Agonising silence

Aiden   Hi Cara… Hi.. Hello… er… Hey there! You're an idiot do not say 'Hey there!'. It's about as good as 'Yo' and if you actually say 'Yo' I'm jumping out of a window.

Angel   Come on, Aiden. You've just got to do it

Aiden   I can't do this. If I just give up on this I'll be much better off really. I'm going to get completely humiliated. Why would she choose me over… Jack?

Angel Because Jack is a moron… and a boy. Cara needs more than that, she needs someone to protect her.

Aiden "Hi Cara, so I'm completely in love with you. Would you like to get married?"

"Oh yeah - let's do that then"

"Oh great - super!"

Urgh. Oh my days. I know how to make her run away.

"Hey, I already know how big your feet are so I bought you these shoes for our wedding. Will you marry me?"

Ok ok… what do girls like? Flowers! Of course they do. That's safe. Who doesn't like flowers?

Right flowers. If we're gonna do this I guess. Go big or go home. Well not that big. Like small flowers that I can actually afford. Like big-small. I'll just walk into a florist and say "Hey have you got any big-small flowers for a girl that doesn't even like me. You do? Great - I'll have some of those please. Yeah I'm desperately in love with her and I'm lonely."

My life.

What are we even doing here Boomer?

Angel   Aiden. You have no idea how unique you are. The first girl that recognises who you are... [frustrated now] You just have to show Cara who you are. You are what every girl wants and doesn't know how to recognise.

Aiden   All I know is that I can't show her who I actually am because all this is definitely *not* cool.

Sorry Ruth. [to the picture]

Aiden moves from the desk to the bed and with comic timing the Angel has to get out of the way hastily as he lays down. Angel ends up on the floor in the least elegant way and has to scramble around to put her glasses back on. As Aiden leaves his desk he leaves behind his pragmatic and logical thoughts. As he lies down on his bed he welcomes in his more dream-like and romantic contemplations...

Aiden   ...it's just that, when I think about her - All I want is a chance to make her happy, I just know that I could make her happy. I would get up every day and try to make her smile at least once in that day. No matter how shitty that day is for her - I just know that I could make her smile just once. She deserves that.

The idea that I could just… I mean we could go to school, do our subjects, get a place a uni…together. Her and me. Me and her. She and I.

Ugh just call her up and be relaxed, Aiden. Be cool. If I only I could just speak to her normally. I just want to be the one who has her back - like ultimately - no matter what. Just give her that space to be her and be part of that…

I wonder what it would be like even?

And I could kiss her… she's so beautiful I think I'd be too scared.

What if I'm actually rubbish at kissing? I mean where do you get kissing lessons? It should be like when you go to the shoe place and you can get your keys done at the same time. You go to a florist and you buy desperation flowers and they point you in the direction of kissing lessons too.

So you get your shoes done, your keys cut, your florist does desperation flowers and kissing lessons and then what… What then? Why isn't there a manual for this? Are you cringing yet Boomer? Cause I am.
Brilliant.

Aiden cuddles and fusses Boomer in a good humoured way.

Aiden *Who's the best? Boomer is the best! Boomer is the best!*

[to Boomer] Boomer I think you're actually too good for me mate. You ought to break up with me. Wait! Is my only good relationship with an adult male dog? Oh my days things are bad. It's worse than I thought. No offence Boom.

[Song 9: Aiden's Song – Solo]

Aiden sings a ballad to express his feeling about Cara.

Act 2

Scene IV: Not Right

Cara and Jack are alone in his bedroom. They are both sober. Jack is trying to initiate a sexual encounter with Cara – who is clearly very uncomfortable, reluctant and unready. Jack has made up his own mind that the time *is* right – at least for him – and that if Cara can get over the trepidation of losing her virginity she'll feel fine about sex – she'll enjoy it.

Jack [counting money] So he was like "and I'll pay you double on Monday" and I was like "As if mate I must look like a mug or something". Damn – I'm not giving bank loans out now… So what d'you

	wanna do Babe? I could get us a takeaway and I don't know [touches her face suggestively] …turn down the lights a bit?
Cara	I just want to chill out and take it easy – it has been a really long day for me. Mr Harris has got it into his head that I've got ability in physics, and he gave me this whole pep talk ages ago – which was cute – but I'm not feeling it and he won't leave it alone and I swear he's just picking on me now 'cos he's angry I'm not doing any work in his lessons. *How is that even fair?*
Jack	Yeah that sounds peak. He probably just fancies you. What a paedo. [teasing] You're too hot for him… [walking fingers up her arm]

Cara	I just want to, like, watch a film or something…
Jack	Why don't you have a drink it might help you relax?
Cara	Probably actually put me to sleep - I just wanna chill…
Jack	You want some weed? That would definitely help you to chill? It'll be the good stuff?
Cara	Not gonna lie - that last time that I had weed I had some really dark thoughts the next day and I didn't feel good about it at all - I am not sure that it's great for me…
Jack	Everyone gets that to begin with and then it just settles down - the secret is just to keep a little bit in your system. Come on babe… [starts trying to kiss

	her neck] you know how you get when you're a little bit high... *it's fun...*
Cara	I'm actually really stressed about school, and I've got a headache – *it's not you*, I'm just not in that place babe... I'm sorry.
Jack	You don't even have to do anything – I'll get you there... you know I'm good at that... I've got some skills [putting a hand clumsily on her boob like some kind of an 'on/off' switch]
Cara	Oh you've got moves babe – but I'm just worn out... [removing his hand] maybe we could fool around a bit this weekend when I'm you know... a bit more *there*... I could wear something that you like?

Jack   You know that you don't have to wear *anything* for me… literally…

Cara   You're sweet… I just…

Jack   What?... [sits up] Are you… rejecting me?

Cara   No! no – it's not like that Jack… oh God. I just have to be honest with you. [Big pause] I never have and I just don't feel ready yet. Just not this evening.

Jack   [moody passive aggressive silence]

Cara   Don't be mad at me. I just don't want my first time to be some hasty thing when I've got a mad headache and my mind is on school and I'm dressed in my skanky school uniform. I kinda… just want it to be… special and romantic. I want it to be *right*.

Jack   It's me, isn't it? *I'm* not right. Fact is that – if *I* was right you'd probably be jumping me right now. I know – I know.

Cara   That is so not what this is.

Jack   You know that we're too old for holding hands right? Like this relationship is either going to get sexual or – let's face it – *we're not going to be together*. Maybe this just isn't right for you at all?

Cara   What are you even saying? It's not like that. You know it's not like that!

Jack   [Moody passive aggressive silence]

Cara   You *know* it's not like that though, right?!

Jack	I don't know anything actually. I mean it's always me that is trying to take this relationship forward and I just don't think you take it seriously. It's never you – it's always me.
Cara	*What do you mean?!* All the things I have done for you – and I'm not talking about sex, I mean *everything*. I thought that there was something emotional between us, not just physical and I have been so committed to that!
Jack	Oh yeah – right – but you just keep me dangling.
Cara	Oh I do not.
Jack	I'm… I'm starting to get the idea that you're just one of those girls.
Cara	What girls?!

Jack   My mates have all warned me.

Cara   Oh my god what?!

Jack   They said you were just a prick tease.

Cara   What the hell would they know about you and me?

Jack's mobile phone message alert sounds. Jack pulls away from Cara. He sits moodily on the edge of the bed with his back to Cara. He takes the message deliberately ignoring her.

Cara   Who is that?

Jack   Who knows – probably just one of those girls who is always chasing me that actually wants a *full* relationship

Cara   Oh that is just not fair! How could you say that?!

Jack reads the text message to himself, which has come from his friend Jon. It reads:

"So have you sealed the deal yet stud? Tick tock mate - time is going by - where's that nasty video??"

Emboldened by the challenge Jack decides that one way or another - tonight *it is* happening.

Cara   You have no idea how hurtful what you just said is. If you've got some dirty slut on your phone maybe you should just go and have some meaningless encounter with her instead of me…

Jack   [messaging back] Standby mate you're not gonna believe what I've got to send you.

          [speaks to Cara] Well maybe that's not the worst advice you can give me. I'm not here to be your little boy that just waits around for a kiss on the cheek. I mean when we move on we can be friends – that's cool – but I'm just not here for a relationship that isn't fulfilling all my needs… and maybe you could get some help then.

Cara   What do you mean?! *What help?*

Jack   Well, it's not my fault you're being frigid – you could be one of those women who has a problem and needs to deal with it. I mean – you said that it's *not me*? I

	mean you said that you're attracted to me right?
Cara	Well yeah I am – of course I am
Jack	And you said that you think I'm hot?
Cara	Yeah…
Jack	And you've put your hands all over me before – but you just can't find the courage to do that last thing and actually, you know…
Cara	Oh my God… [pause] *maybe you're right?* [tears]
Jack	It's ok. You're just not ready for this type of a relationship. I still respect you for being honest. You'll be ready in time. We can both move on…
Cara	Oh my god you actually are breaking up with me aren't you? [feeling urgent and desperate]

Jack   Look I wanted it to be really special for you too. I'm going to be honest with you… I've had sex with more than one other girl. I have. None of it meant anything – it was just *fun*. It was casual. I was just fucking those girls. I wanted this to be my first time that meant anything… I want to… I wanted to… I guess I was just wrong and you're not that girl

[Jack turns away cynically and puts his hands to his face as if dealing with the tears – wiping them away]

Cara   Jack, Jack – this is going to happen for us – I want this as

	much as you do – that's exactly what I want too, I just…
Jack	Look – the right moment? As far as I'm concerned – it's not about flowers or chocolates or hearts and what we're wearing – it's just when you are with me and we are alone.
Cara	Right… I get that… but…
Jack	There isn't gonna be a time when this isn't worrying for you and it doesn't feel like a big deal – it's your first time
Cara	Yeah… I get that too… but
Jack	And you shouldn't *punish* me just because this isn't my first time – that's not my fault…
Cara	I'm not, I'm not I swear to you!
Jack	Look – I'm sorry to be like this with you Cara – but it really is

	now... *or it's not at all* and that is just how I feel right?
Cara	Oh, well...
Jack	Cara, just reach out your hand to me and don't say anything – *I will do the rest*
Cara	But Jack... I don't want to...
Jack	Shhh – just reach out to me and lay down... shhhh

Jack puts a finger on Cara's mouth to silence her protestations. He knows that nothing she is about to say is going to carry his wishes forward. Instead, he pushes her gently but assertively backwards down into a reclined position on the bed. She doesn't reach out – but her protestations are subdued... she lays rigidly as he begins to kiss her neck and his hand moves to her breasts through her clothing as his fumbling become more determined.

The house lights go down and obscures what happens next. Outside on the street a solitary figure stands in a lonely street light. He takes a long draw on a cigarette and flicks the spent filter into the night air.

The Devil	They grow up so fast. He didn't even need me to be there for him. I'm so proud. That's my boy.

Act 2

Scene V: *Jack - ass*

Jack is out on the street, his general behaviour by now is more ragged and he seems even more irrational and extroverted than ever before. He's living on superficial wealth and arrogance. The fact that he hasn't been arrested has made him even less wary of the risk of being arrested.

Girl 1   Do you have any weed?

Jack   Sure I do – the *best* weed – I got you...

Girl 1   The thing is… *[she looks down before looking up with big eyes]* I don't get paid until Friday baby.. can you help a girl out? I would be so, so, grateful… *[she tilts her head flirtatiously and runs her tongue over her top lip with a wink]*

Jack   *[drapes his hands over her hips while he tucks one little bag of green herbal substance into her cleavage]* now that little bit is on me and maybe I can see you later? You know me right…

Girl 1   Yeah. Thanks babe

A young boy, Junior, enters and approaches Jack. He is a Year 7 who has just come up from Primary School. He is wearing a distinctive jacket with a very particular logo, design, and colour scheme on it that should be instantly recognisable as his. He runs up to Jack eagerly and seems to be craving his approval. He definitely sees Jack as a role model and a leader. He offers Jack a bespoke fist bump that is their 'secret' handshake.

Junior   I got that package out for you. You're so right! The cops never look at me and I just cycle by them like nothing. I got it to the address and he gave me this to give to you.

Jack   Good lad – you're my boy right? [tucking the envelope into his bag] You're in my crew ok. Now what did I tell you were the rules of being in the crew?

Junior It's ok Jack – I remember – er… don't ever tell anyone about the crew, er… never hand over a package before you get the money… erm.. *and wait I can remember this one…* If I ever get found with anything on me I tell them… I found it and I was taking it to my Mum. If they ask me where I found it I take them somewhere random. Right?

Jack   That's right - you're a streetwise kid - you're a real natural. Ok so I got two more things to teach you right now ok?

Junior   Right? Cool!

Jack   Ok so you ever get stopped by anyone - I mean anyone - and they try to search you or put their hands on you - you scream 'PAEDO' at the top of your voice! You got that? You scream "HELP THIS PAEDO TOUCHED ME! HE'S TOUCHING ME!" - they will jump back and *you run*. It doesn't matter where - just as fast as you can - over fences, garages, through back gardens - and you just keep running right?

Junior   Yeah! I got that. I'm really fast!

Jack   Now the other thing you need to know is – no matter what – no matter who – you do not tell anyone about me or anyone else in the crew. OK? *You never snitch*. We're your family and you ain't gonna get that anywhere else. That's how it is – that's how it will always be. Nobody will ever snitch on you and if anyone tries to hurt you we've got your back. So you must never betray these boys out here because we love you man. You got that?

Junior   Yeah – I got it. *[They do their fist bump]*

Jack   Right then - good man - you're gonna be the top boy one day. You're gonna be in charge when I'm done. Now here… this is for you to enjoy with your mates, and this is to buy yourself something with yeah? Don't let anyone see that twenty though because you can't say where it came from, so fold it up and put it inside your phone case, right? Go and enjoy yourself, if I need you I'll call you…

Jack hands Junior a joint made out of low grade weed that he has scraped together and a twenty-pound note.

Junior Thanks Jack!

[Junior exits] Jack checks his shoulder in a conspicuous way, he spits on the ground and adjusts his baseball cap. An unknown person walks through, and they fist bump and shake hands. In one movement a transaction is performed. Two police officers are standing off side of the stage [possibly in the auditorium] and without attempting to disguise themselves, they observe what is an obvious drug deal taking place in a children's playground. Jack goes back into his bag and rearranges his merchandise taking out a scale, a knife, a roll of money and a bag of wrapped cannabis. He is completely unaware of the police officers walking towards him — he has his back to them — it seems certain that he is about to be caught. As this happens, Junior runs back through chasing *a football and as he runs through he deliberately kicks the ball past Jack and makes a hand signal that looks like 'FIVE O' (five fingers and an 'ok' sign'). He mouths "FIVE O FIVE O" at Jack who, throws everything back into his rucksack in a haphazard way. To give him some time and to try to distract the cops Junior throws himself into an improvised distraction:*

Junior   Hey mister, are you guys cops yeah?

PC Wilson   [trying to look past Junior, frustrated at the interruption] Yeah son what's up?

Junior   Can I be a cop? I wannabe a cop one day like you

PC Wilson   You just have to work hard at school and you can be.

Junior   Can I put your helmet on and get a selfie with you?

PC Wilson   Of course, you can, quickly though [he smiles and kneels down taking off his helmet]

PC Clarke   Look I'll take the photo for you ok?

With Junior distracting the cops, Jack repacks his bag and puts a lot of stuff on top of the incriminating gear – hoping that he won't be searched.

He sends an emergency message to Cara and he hopes that she picks it up quickly.

Displayed on a screen above the stage, it reads

'Bring the bag I gave you to the park now! Can't explain. Blue all over me'.

He's about to try to get away from there – walk not run – when the police see him. The situation looks pretty bleak.

PC Wilson   'Scuse me son – yeah – I just saw something that I thought looked a bit conspicuous and we've been told there is drug dealing going on down here at the park…

Jack   What down here? Scum! Nah, I've never seen it but if I did I would say…

PC
Merry

Well I'm sure you'll understand why I need to search you then?

Jack

Well, I mean, you know I kind of need to be away – *will this take long?*

PC
Wilson

Well it takes how long it takes… so first of all we are obliged to tell you that you are being detained for the purpose of a search. I am PC Wilson from Sandford Police Station and this is my colleague PC Clarke. This search will be recorded and you are entitled to a copy of the search record – we can email that to you if you give us your email address or phone number, alternatively you can collect a copy of this record for up to one year at your local police station. *Do you understand?*

PC Wilson   I need to make you aware, before we go any further, that you do not have to say anything, but it may harm your defence if you do not mention when questioned, something which you later rely on in court — anything you do say, may be given in evidence? *Do you understand?*

Jack   What are you nicking me??!!

PC Clarke   No no — it's ok — it just means that anything you say can be recorded and offered in court if we found anything and a case was brought to trial. You understand that this is all being captured on body worn video. You don't have to answer our questions – but if you don't and you later decide to answer the same question in court it might look shady – ok?

Jack   Look, look this is getting pretty heavy – *I haven't done anything at all…*

Cara and the Devil enter from opposite sides of the stage. Cara has clocked what is going on. She is carrying a rucksack that is identical to the one being held by Jack. Her job is to try a very risky manoeuvre but as she is working out how to do it, the Devil (smartly dressed and looking very business-like with a briefcase in hand) walks right into the middle of the police engagement.

The Devil: Gentlemen, officers, – I am so sorry to distract you – this is a bit of an emergency… could you tell me where the Sandford Oaks Care Home for the Elderly is please? I'm a doctor and I must get there as soon as possible?

PC Clarke: Well yes of course – you go down to the bottom and turn left

The Devil: Right you say.? Sorry you must speak up I'm rather *death* you see

PC Wilson: No he said left – LEFT – at the bottom you go LEFT

PC Clarke   [begins pointing and giving signals]

Junior   Hey mister how do you get so good at being a cop anyway?

PC Clarke   Well it's all about keeping your wits about you – you never take your eye off the ball you know?

The officers turn their back on Jack for just a moment. Recognising this golden opportunity, Cara needs no invitation… she spirits into position and switches the two rucksacks without a word. She doesn't even seem to acknowledge Jack and the whole transaction is made with silent efficiency. As she moves away from Jack, Cara fears she was seen by PC Wilson, and she offers him a cheeky wink and a flirtatious gesture. PC Wilson acknowledges with a wry smile and speaks quietly to PC Clarke covering his radio:

PC Wilson   I've still got it with the girls mate.

PC Clarke   Shut up it's the uniform.

PC Wilson   Well I don't see anyone winking at you.

PC Clarke   Your Mum winks at me all the time.

PC Wilson   My Mum has a nervous tick around weirdos.

Jack   Er, erm, Officers – sorry I really need to get going did you need to search me? *[offering open palms and proffering the innocent rucksack]*

PC Wilson   Yeah – let's get this finished ok… sorry son… so where were we?

The formalities of the now frustrated search fall quiet as the actors playing Wilson, Clarke and Jack mime out the rest of the event in silence, including a full pat down. Instead, our attention is drawn across to Cara who, in her urgency to get away, encounters Aiden [enters] – without recognising him or looking at where she is going at all. Aiden is holding a modest, pretty, and understated bunch of flowers and he is making his way directly towards

Cara – whom he clearly wants to give them to. He is feeling incredibly conspicuous – as if everyone is about to burst out laughing at him. They collide in a clumsy way, the flowers are knocked out of his hands and Cara inadvertently walks directly through them. She is full of adrenaline and desperate to get away.

Cara rounds the corner of a prominent wall and doubles over. She begins to vomit through her natural anxiety. Wiping her mouth, she sinks to the ground and sits with her knees up to her chest, trying to regulate her breathing – she is hyperventilating.

On the opposite side of the wall Aiden gives up trying to collect the trampled flowers, and instead he sits, with his back to the same wall – feeling humiliated, and wordlessly contemplating the apparent rejection that he has just suffered. The two characters sit back-to-back reflecting away from each other.

Cara's phone alerts her to a call, the number shows up on the wall at the back of the stage it says "Sandford Oaks Care Home for the Elderly". She shakes her head and diverts it to answer service.

Act 2
Scene V: *Granddad II*

Granddad sits alone in his room. He shivers and looks across to his bed, where his blanket is. He looks down and thinks about the effort it will take to go and get that. He looks across at the blanket again. A large clock is projected on the wall. It never seems to move. The seconds hand shivers occasionally like it might tick – but it lacks the energy – and time never passes. He looks at the clock. He hopes that Cara might arrive. He stretches out a shaking hand and takes down a picture of the two of them that he keeps beside him. He is younger and Cara is a child. Holding the photo in the frame he looks at it and smiles. He wipes his eyes, trying to shrug away the tears. He chastises himself:

Granddad You silly old fool. She's got a life you know. She's probably got a boyfriend now. You don't need your old Granddad when you've got a boyfriend. You silly old fool.

The low thump of a rap beat with heavy bass reverberates in his room from a car on the road outside. It feels hostile, like the approach of a predator, and it surrounds and disorientates him. He frowns and shivers again. He looks over to the blanket. The rap beat is just rhythm and bass - no melody. It is a deep and dark dubstep beat.

Granddad   Come on. You're too dependent on people. You're a burden. You can't make people do everything for you.

Granddad gets up out of his chair – it takes him a couple of goes to find his feet and he stops for his breath. He starts to move with agonising progress towards the blanket, planning a route that allows him to lean on as many pieces of furniture as possible.

Granddad   That's it. Slowly. Good lad.

Granddad stops. On the floor there is a cup and a plate. Does he try to navigate round them? Does he try to bend down to lift them up? Does he knock them over? Why are they even there? He looks at them for a long time. He looks back towards the blanket. He thinks about giving up and going back to his chair - but he has come so far. He looks at the chair. He looks at the blanket again. He frowns. Granddad decides to try and walk through the obstacle.

Granddad   [He knocks over the cup which has tea in it.] You messy sod. Now look!

Unsteady he almost loses balance - panics slightly - the last time he fell he had to go to hospital and everyone was mad at him and told him he was silly for not looking after himself properly. He places a hand on his chest. He bends over slightly and takes some air. He notices his wedding photo just there.

Grandad   Hello you. I haven't seen you for a while. How are you gorgeous? Look at the state of me eh? Look at this. You wouldn't have married this! You were the most beautiful girl I ever saw. I'll see you again soon. [Pauses] It won't be long.

Granddad finally makes it to the blanket. It feels like an odyssey. He smiles gently in triumph. He stretches out his shaking arms. He picks up the blanket – which seems heavy… he feels it all over… it's damp. It's cold and damp. It doesn't smell good. Granddad remembers. It was all for nothing.

Granddad   Ah well. [exhales and looks at his bed]

Granddad sits back down into his chair awkwardly as he hears what he thinks is the noise of the door – or maybe it was just next door…

Granddad   Cara?! Is that you? Is that you my love? [pause] Are you there?

Exhausted, Granddad falls into a slumber. In the background, the Devil has entered. He is dressed as he was on the street in the scene prior. He carries a briefcase which he opens at the front of the stage. Out of it, he pulls a white Doctor's coat and a stethoscope, both of which he puts on slowly and deliberately. He moves quietly and with a sinister air. Granddad doesn't notice him. The Devil walks across the room to a box next to Granddad's chair which he opens. It is full of clean blankets. He shakes his head and smiles in pity. He takes one blanket out and puts it over Granddad as if preparing him.

He then approaches the table in the room. He picks up a knife and a set of rosary beads. Dropping the rosary beads into his pocket, he crosses the room with ease and with noiseless stealth. He runs his finger across the blade of the knife and nicks his finger. He makes an 'ooh' face and smiles with the corners of his mouth. He sucks at the blood on his finger and rubs the tips of his fingers together. He looks at the knife and he looks at Granddad. He looks into the audience. He smiles.

The Devil   Let's play a little game. If she picks up the phone, I'll leave. I promise. But I bet she won't. [Pauses] I do love a little game.

The Devil dials on the telephone, slowly and deliberately, prolonging the tension… the ring tone sounds throughout the auditorium and collectively, we hope that Cara will pick up. All she has to do is answer the phone.

The Devil   Nobody can say I'm not fair.

The phone continues to ring – and the Devil plays with the coiled wire on the landline phone, but there is no answer… and then it is diverted to voicemail.

Voicemail This is voicemail for 07700900465 You can leave a message after this bleep.

The Devil Well, I guess it is what it is.
[faux shake of the head]

The Devil sighs with mock resignation and tilts his head to one side in an empty gesture of sympathy.

The Devil Thoughts and prayers old man. This never gets any easier.

Granddad is asleep in his bed. He moves in his sleep and rolls slightly but in an awkward way that discomforts him. The Devil takes the knife over to Granddad and he runs the tip of the knife under his throat and gently across his throat as if he is seeking out the jugular vein. The tickling sends Granddad into a coughing fit.

The Devil [Whispers to Granddad as he is coughing] That's it you silly old fool. It's time. You're right you know. She *has* got a boyfriend and I'll be honest, I don't think he even loves her. He just uses her for sex. He's got her doing drugs now. She's running in the street with him *right now*. Helping him to get away from the cops. She gets drunk with him. I can't say for sure – but… I think she's in *love* with him. And that's why she's not here. And that's why she didn't answer the phone.

It's so simple. *She loves him more than you.*

Granddad *[coughing fit escalates and it becomes difficult to breathe as he coughs he clutches his chest]*

The Devil *[Slips the knife into his pocket]* Glancing towards the door he places a gloved hand over the old man's mouth and he leans with his body weight into Granddad's face.

[Muffled alarm from Granddad and strobe lighting as the life leaves his body]

The Devil Shhhh it's ok old man there's nothing to stay here for, it's time now… trust me… *I'll get you out of her way…*

[Stops struggling and he lays very, very still- the strobe lighting stops]

The Devil [Removes his glove and touches the jugular vein with two fingers and looks at his watch. He frowns in approval, nodding slightly. He puts his glove back on and checks his watch]

Time of death… *who the fuck cares?*

[He allows himself a grim smile. He turns to the audience] Shhh –

don't tell. Snitches get stitches yeah?

The Devil walks casually out of the care flat and on his way he tugs on the alarm cord, smiles at the audience, climbs out the window and exits as the care home staff begin to arrive in numbers rushing through the door.

INTERVAL

Act 3

Act 3

Scene I – *Pregnant*

Jack's room. It's dark and gloomy, lit blue by the stage lights to create a cold, crude atmosphere. The room is barely put together with peeling wallpaper, a stained bedsheet sprawled over Jack's bed revealing the mattress underneath, open draws with clothes spilling out from them, graffiti on the walls, a lamp with no lampshade perched on the floor by the bed and a broken TV discarded by a door splintering under the damage of several punch marks.

Cara and Jack are lying in Jack's dirty bed which is positioned sideways on the stage. There is silence. Jack is sat upright and rests his back against the headboard whilst texting on his phone.

Cara lies on her side with her back towards Jack. She's facing the audience but she's not looking at them - instead staring blankly into the distance. She looks manhandled: her hair scruffy and bedraggled, mascara smudged, arms bruised and dark circles so deep her eyes look hollow. Worn down and dejected- there's a thin blanket on the bed to cover herself with so she wraps her own arms around her body and holds herself. The silence is palpable and painful.

A voicemail message begins to play across the theatre. Cara lies rigid and unblinking. She gives no indication that she can hear it.

Voicemail	You have one new message and zero saved messages. New message:
Cara's Dad (Voice)	[angry] Cara- it's your Dad. We've been trying to get hold of you for hours now. You didn't come home last night again. Where are you? We figured you were at Hannah's house but not for this long. Are you even coming home tonight? [his approach changes now: his tone softer and more concerned] Come on Cara. We're worried about you. [pause] So worried. [another uncomfortable pause - he doesn't know what to say] Look love, I know I haven't always been there for

> you but I'm here now and I miss you. We miss you. [long pause] Talk soon. Bye.

The line goes dead. Silence.

Jack then puts down his phone and swings his legs over to sit on the side of the bed, his back to the audience. He coughs foully before standing up and selecting a t-shirt from a pile of clothes on the floor. He sniffs it for a moment before shrugging and putting it on. Without saying a word to Cara, he picks up his phone from the bed, another phone from the floor, a stained jacket, and his rucksack before leaving the room.
Once she is sure Jack has left, Cara's gaze unfixes from the back of the theatre, and she sits up slowly and

deliberately – as though the action is agonising. Arms now wrapped around her stomach, she puts her head between her knees and sits in silence for an uncomfortably long time. She then leans over the side of the bed to find her schoolbag which she rifles through for a moment before pulling out a pregnancy test. She curses under her breath. With tears in her eyes, she drags herself off the bed and off the stage. Whilst she is off stage, the Angel enters.
After an uncomfortably long silence, Cara re-enters the stage.

Cara   Shit, shit, shit, shit...please no, please no. I can't do this. I'm not ready. [groans angrily] It wasn't supposed to happen like this! Things were supposed to be different. I was supposed to do my GCSEs, go to college, get into Uni, then a job, a partner, maybe get married, and *then* this. I know no one does it like that anymore but that's what I wanted. It's all backwards now. I can't do this. [pause] Oh Cara you're so evil for not wanting this. Some people would give everything to have what you have right now - *you can't be so ungrateful*. This is what you've always wanted...*just not right now*. I mean, of course, I would love it with everything that

I am, but that's not enough. Love isn't enough now.

How am I meant to keep us safe if I can't even keep *myself* safe? Because of me, it will grow up in *this* world - constantly scared that the next knock at the door will be the police, or someone you owe money to, with a knife ready to kill you right there and then. I can't get out now. I'd have nothing.

I'd... be… nothing.

Cara sinks down onto her knees in front of the pregnancy test. The Angel walks silently onto the stage and places his hand comfortingly onto Cara's shoulder. Cara continues without acknowledging the

Angel's presence. She can't see or feel her.

Cara   Even if I did get out, where would I go? Dad would be so disappointed in me. Mum would kick me out for sure and I can't stay with Grandad.

              Jack is my life. But is he really the type of guy to stick around? I don't look great now but I won't look any better in nine months, and he won't like that. He won't like me anymore.

              Oh god, how am I supposed to tell him? I know I shouldn't

get ahead of myself, *I don't even know for sure yet.*

But...I do know *really*. Deep down. I've had all the symptoms...every single one and I don't know but I can just...feel it. *[pause]* But I don't want this.

This can't happen. I'm completely and utterly on my own. I can't...

Loud beeping echoes throughout the theatre. Her three minutes are up. Cara is frozen. We wait with bated breath. Eventually, she reluctantly leans forward and peers at the result.

It is positive.

She is pregnant. This isn't shown explicitly to the audience, but her following reaction should make the result obvious.

Cara   I can't… have this baby.

She dissolves. The Angel wraps his arms around her but it's almost futile - she can't feel or believe that he's there. After a few moments, her phone rings. Illuminated on the screen behind her, we can see that it is "Sandford Oaks Care Home". Cara wipes her eyes, sniffs and picks up her phone.

Cara   [frustrated] Oh god, not now!

She hangs up in silence.

Angel   You need to call someone

Cara   I need to tell Jack...

She pauses. On the screen behind her, we see a list of her recent contacts: (top to bottom) Stanford Oaks Care Home, Jack, Aidan, Dad, Mum.
We are willing her to realise that it's Aiden that she needs.
Cara opts to send a message to Jack ["I've got something important to tell you – see you at yours – 4PM ok?"]
Cara pulls her knees against her chest. The Angel strokes her hair and looks at her in a sorrowful way. A gentle beat and a melody begin to swell – the beat resembles her heartbeat at first, a lighter secondary beat resembles that of a child within her...

[Song 10: Angel's song]

Angel's song begins as a solo to Cara – a song of reassurance and sympathy. It shows compassion for Cara and her situation and promises not to judge her – but to support her.

Cara can't hear the song and appears not to be lifted by it.

The song moves into a rousing gospel arrangement based around a memorable chorus and a choir join with upbeat harmonies and a full instrumental accompaniment brings the whole piece to a climax.

Cara dries her eyes and starts to feel stronger and more positive – as if she can face the future.

[Stage lights go down and the scene ends.]

Act 3
Scene II - *Confidence*

The scene opens with Cara sitting alone on a park bench looking pensive. She has a lot on her mind. Despite being in a relationship with Jack, she still doesn't feel that she has a friendship or anyone she can confide in. Aiden enters the scene and discovers her unexpectedly. He practises a few robotic approaches that he might use to casually approach her - miming these to the amusement of the audience. He shakes his head "no" and his frustration grows. As his behaviour becomes more conspicuous and odd, inevitably Cara turns her head and notices a slightly bizarre display that resembles some kind of French street artist having an existential crisis in Sandford park.

Cara   Are… you ok Aiden?

Aiden *[Embarrassed at the discovery and not knowing how long Cara has been watching]* Yup. Fine. Fine. No problem. I didn't see you there. Sorry Cara… I'm… thinking about...

The Devil walks through quickly and whispers a line in his ear, Aiden blurts it out without even thinking

Aiden …changing my identity and becoming a zookeeper

Cara   Er what?

Aiden   Sorry I meant… er… joining the amateur dramatics club at school. People who do school plays are never weird and they're always really popular right?

Aiden/actor looks out into the audience for some kind of acknowledgement of this meta joke.

Cara   Ok so you're being really weird… *[to herself]* but at least you're honest.

Aiden   Can I… er… Can I sit with you?

Cara   *[Looks at him like he's even more odd now]* Well a tramp was sitting there a minute ago and he might have pissed himself – but if I'm worth sitting in piss for, then, yeah… go on then.

Aiden   I'll actually take that.

Aiden sits down and the look on his face tends to suggest that – just maybe – Cara wasn't lying.

Aiden   Ok – I kinda hoped you were joking, and I'm not gonna lie, this seat actually is wet – so there's a 50/50 chance that I'm sitting in tramp's piss

Cara   Hate to break it to you mate, there's a 90/10 chance that you're sitting in a tramp's piss and that's only because the other 10% is pure alcohol. Trust me I heard him exhale when he did it.

Aiden I've had better days.

Cara Me too. And I'm not gonna lie – I'd actually swap. Not seats obviously, but days. You can keep the seat.

Aiden Why is your day going so bad?

Cara Like you wanna know right? What are you listening to?

Aiden You... you won't like it. *It's not rap.*

Cara I do like other music, you know.

Aiden Yeah but... I don't know...

Cara   [Mock seriousness] Oh so you think you're too good for me now Aiden?

Aiden   [Reluctantly takes one earphone out and slowly hands it to Cara] Ok, but I told you it was kind of lame…

[Song 11: Granddad and Cara's Duet (Reprise)]

As Cara puts the earphone into her ear, and they share the headphones, a mono version of the tune that she used to listen to with her grandfather fills her mind with beautiful and fond memories of the past and a special relationship – a closeness that she cannot begin to replace. Hearing the music is confusing and painful.

Granddad enters and dances across the stage as Aiden falls inanimate beside her. Granddad's late wife, Cara's Nana, follows him and they move across the stage and are gone as quickly as they had arrived. Only Cara can absorb this vision and her face drops into an expressionless stare, her eyes are fixed into an indeterminate distance. She is hit profoundly by the music and this creation of her mind in a way that Aiden cannot understand - he is fearful that his music has seriously undermined his credibility in her eyes.

Cara cannot fathom how this would be something that Aiden would listen to. She is rendered into a serious state of mind. She speaks frankly and directly to Aiden in a way that contrasts her earlier and more playful tone. She is suddenly very serious . – but more open:

Cara   Why would you want to know what happened to me?

Aiden Er… I might not be a complete monster?

Cara   Well… I really don't know if I can actually even bring myself to say it. I'm not exactly what you'd call a sharer.

Aiden Alright – I'm not after your last Malteser – it doesn't have to be your life story. It better be embarrassing because at the moment I am definitely 1-0 down. *[The joke falls flat with Cara and emphasises that the mood has definitely changed, they are not joking now]*

Cara   *[Seems to come back to the surface and now looks at Aiden with an apologetic smile and warmth in her eyes that has a genuine effect on Aiden that she doesn't comprehend]* Look… *[her tone gets very serious]* you can't tell anyone and I'm not even joking right?

Aiden   Of course.

Cara   Right... So… Jack is dealing. And he's got me doing stuff too. *Not like that.* I mean, like that, but not *like that.* You know what I mean? Please tell me you know what I mean...

Aiden   I kinda do, yeah… *[He doesn't]*

Cara   Ok and it actually scares me. He's not as good at this stuff as he likes to think that he is and if he gets careless we're going to prison Aiden. *I can't go to prison.* There's a really good reason why I can't go to prison. Well. A really bad reason. Well. I don't even know what kind of reason. I don't even know any more.

Aiden   Cara there's no such thing as a good reason to go to prison.

Cara   That's not what I meant! I mean there's a reason I can't get put away and… I don't know if that's a good thing or a bad thing.

Aiden Well if it means you can't get put away it's a good thing – surely?

Cara I don't think you understand

Aiden What don't I understand?

Cara [Pause] I'm pregnant.

There is a long silence. They both sit in the moment and it's hard to pretend that this is good news. It crystalises that whether Cara keeps the baby or not – these are definitely not happy circumstances and really, Cara doesn't want to be a Mum and she isn't ready. The enormity of what has happened is bearing down on Cara and she collapses sideways into Aiden, suddenly crying in an outpouring that she has been suppressing for some time. Aiden doesn't know what to do, but instinctively puts an arm around Cara - but holds her delicately - and hardly dares to breathe in case it might provoke Cara to realise that he is actually holding her. He is scared that she might withdraw. Cara has her head on Aiden's chest as if she is shielded by it and she is hiding in it. To Cara, Aiden feels warm and protective on the most cold and inhospitable evening.

Cara   I'm only 15! Aiden! I'm only 15 what the hell am I gonna do?! Are they gonna lock Jack up? He knew I wasn't 16. That's rape right? Are they gonna lock him up? *Rapists go to prison*. Child rapists go to prison. Drug dealers go to prison - that's all I've ever been told. That's all I've ever heard. I don't want to be the reason that Jack goes to prison for rape. The police hate him. What's gonna happen when they find out - will they question me?! Do I *have* to tell them who the father is? Will they do a paternity test? I mean what? "Hi Jack, these police officers are here to give you the news that you raped me?!"

Aiden We can work this out Cara...

Cara I don't know what to say. Who to tell. There is nobody to talk to.

Aiden   You can always talk to me… because… you've known me forever. I remember you from when we first started at Primary School together – you remember that? We both started the term late and we were like the new kids right? And we were so small, and I thought it was just me and you were so cool about it and I was struggling and you just looked after me.

Cara   Yeah you were pretty lame not gonna lie. *[sniffing]*

Aiden   Oh yeah – laugh it up – it's really funny!

Cara Sorry! *[still sniffing and wiping her eyes]*

Aiden Yeah well – you know, I know we went in separate directions a bit – I never forgot that. I never lost sight of you… it was kinda sad that we stopped talking though. I wanted to talk to you but I thought it would be weird… I thought I was weird and that you might think so too.

Cara I missed you too though…

Aiden I really missed you… because… like… since then I've never met anyone who actually could be as considerate or as kind as you are. You never put yourself first…

Cara   Stop it…

Aiden   I mean it. You don't and I see that Cara. I'm not going to lie - it has been really hard. You've not seemed happy - I don't mean to be rude or to pry - but I'm not weird or anything, but I have noticed because… I do look and… I do see…

Because you mean a lot more than you realise to… people… and definitely to… someone who went to primary school with you… Look I gotta say this now because I just feel like if I don't say this now I will never have the courage to ever say it again and I'm just so scared after this you might not ever talk to me again, so I just have to say it ok? Just forgive me if I'm out of line because I would never want to upset you Cara…

But…Jack is just not good for you right? [the 'I love you' crescendo flattens as Aiden swerves what he really wanted to say yet again]

Jack gets all his money on the street dealing drugs and that is just not you. He makes money selling addiction and dependency problems on behalf of a criminal gang who brutalise this whole neighbourhood and make everyone feel scared. He is always whistling at the next girl that walks past him and he never gives you respect in public and he never has your back… and I don't know a lot but I know enough to see that this isn't gonna end well because he's not gonna be useful to this crew forever and then they're gonna get rid of him one way or another and that hurt and that harm is going to come back to you. I mean I would never wish ill on anyone – not even Jack – because he doesn't know any better, but I can't just watch you get hurt in all this too Cara because you ought to know by now, you really need to know that…

Jack enters the scene and sees Cara sharing earphones and in close physical contact with Aiden who is pouring out his heart to her. He can see that Cara is absolutely connected on a level that is more than just physical – and the worst part of it is

they're not kissing and groping each other
– this is not casual messing about. Jack is
struck deeply by a genuine and jealous pain
of seeing his girlfriend making an
emotional connection with another boy.

Jack   What the fuck is all this then?! *[He strikes Aiden immediately to the side of the head from behind with an open palm, slapping him violently off the park bench and to the ground in shock]*

Aiden   Jack!

Jack   Yeah – *fuck* you Aiden *[Jack produces a knife quickly from his pocket]*

Cara   Don't hurt him Jack! Please! Just no… this isn't whatever it looks like

Jack   You lying little slag! It didn't take you long once you got off the mark did it?

Jack grabs a handful of Cara's hair. She screams in pain as he pulls her off the bench.

Aiden   Jack no - you've got no right

Jack   *Fuck you* - what you gonna do? You want some of this? You see that Cara? That little pussy won't do anything. Is that what you want? A little pussy boy that won't step up for you? Look at him! Look at him! Open your eyes!

Jack begins to drag Cara to the side exit of the stage as if he is leaving with his property – but before he exits, he stops…

Jack   You think this little crew are going to ruin me Aiden? You don't know me mate. I'm gonna own this whole crew in a couple of months mate. I'm gonna take out their boss, I'm gonna take them down and then they'll all be making money for me. You think I'm happy to be making a cut on the street? You think I'm gonna be out here hustling a dot five of weed here and there? No mate – I've got my plans. That boss is a *pussy boy* and I'm gonna see to him and once that's out of the way I'm going to start making some very real money. I've got my plans. And by then Aiden, you'll be doing your fucking bin round or sweeping up the shit in school because you're a *nothing*.

As Jack continues with his pronouncements, he rubs his nose frantically, and at the side of the stage the Devil discreetly sits with a mobile phone in hand. He's recording the speech and the events. As Jack finishes and exits the stage – pulling Cara by the hair – the Devil calmly pushes the button to finish his recording. He presses a few buttons, and the footage is sent via a social media feed directly into the County Lines gang which is shown to the audience on a screen above the stage. Satisfied with himself, he gives a grim smile. He puts the phone away into his pocket and walks casually from the stage in the opposite direction. Aiden is gathering himself together and making sense of everything that has just happened as the scene closes.

Act 3
Scene III – *Coercive Control*

Jack marches Cara through his bedroom door – holding her by the arm. They've just been in the park and he believes that he 'caught her' with Aiden being unfaithful.

Jack   [*throws Cara to the floor by her arm violently*] You're nothing but a dirty sket you know that?

Cara   [*shocked*] What did I do?

Jack   Do you know what my reputation is worth out there? How you made me look? I bet you did it on purpose! You want my money, you want the drink and the drugs don't you? You want me to give you the good life and all that – all the things… You're out there with every boy that walks by and gives you the time of day like a whore. *Even that little dick Aiden*

Cara   He's not a dick!

Jack   It's like that is it?!

Cara   What? You're *mental!*

Jack   *[shouting]* I'm mental am I? You're out there sharing headphones with some pathetic little loser. It's not even like you were sitting with someone I could respect – that *anyone* could respect. You can't fancy him?! Aiden?! It's like you want people to laugh at me. What is the most humiliating thing in the whole world? Your girl getting off with another bloke behind your back. *Nah – your girl getting off with some pathetic little loser in the middle of a park where everyone can see it...*

Jack breaks something and punches a wall as his anger begins to escalate

Cara   Stop it! You're scaring me

Jack   *I'm scaring you am I?!* Am I?! You should've fucking thought about that shouldn't you?! Why didn't you think about that? It's because you're thick! That's why!

Cara   What? Where is this coming from? I've never seen you like this before!

Jack   Well get used to it darling because if you want to play stupid games you win stupid prizes!

Cara   I'm not staying here to take this!

Jack   *You bet you are!* Get back down there where I put you!

Jack strikes Cara viciously across the face with the back of his hand. Cara is propelled backwards in pain and in shock. She goes to the floor. She is crying and is very scared now. Jack is getting more and more angry. She has the presence of mind to run into the bathroom and lock the door. She sits with her back to the door. Already waiting inside the room is The Angel.

Jack   *[Bangs on the door hard]* This is me now you bitch – and you'd better look to like it!

Cara   I'll look to like it if looking liking move! You're a monster!

Jack   *The fuck is that supposed to even mean even?! Are you tryna make me look thick? look what you turned me into! Look what you made me do! Do you think I want to have to hit you? Look at you – why did you have to cause all this? You slag, you... little slag... [he breaks something else and starts crying]*

Cara is on the floor – her knees are drawn up to her chest, her back is to the wall, she is listening to Jack and his rage, as he breaks things, in absolute fear, but she dare not move from where she is. There are tears running down her face. The locked door is the only safety that she has – and every now and again he punches or kicks at it, and she jumps as if she has received an electric shock. She is scared that he might be able to get through the door to her…

The Angel is crouched down with her and puts her hands over Cara's ears in a comfort gesture to protect her from the harmful noise and language that the door cannot muffle.

As Cara is hidden behind the bathroom door, the Devil enters the outer room and he sits on the bed near Jack. Neither Jack nor Cara show any awareness of him being there at all..

Devil   [Whispers something that the audience can't hear into Jack's ear]

Jack   [As Jack runs out of rage] Oh shit – what have I done? I'm sorry Cara, I'm sorry Baby. I'm so sorry. I'm sorry. *[he paws at the door pathetically, scratching like a dog that wants to be let in]*

Cara *[Attempting to de-escalate him and maybe talk her way out]* It's ok, it's fine - it was my fault - I just need a minute ok. Just, just give me a minute. I'll be fine.

Devil *[nods in satisfaction as he smirks, he whispers again into Jack's ear]*

Jack I promise you - this will never happen again - *we'll both* learn from this. It doesn't ever have to happen again Baby. You just don't know what you mean to me, that's all.

[silence - the use of dramatic silences between them is extremely important in this scene once Jack calms down and becomes more manipulative. From here The Angel has her hands over Cara's ears to protect her and she 'zones out']

Devil   *[Pulls out a notepad that he is scribbling in. He makes a face like 'might work'. He whispers into Jack's ear again.]*

Jack   You see, all I want is to find a life for us. I never knew that I could actually love anyone until I met you - I've never had any love in my life. Then you came along. I don't know anything about any of this.

Devil   [*Less than satisfied, shakes his head, shrugs, time for a different tac… whispers again into Jack's ear*]

Jack   I would never hurt you - it's just the stress out there on the street. I only it for us. I want to build us a life - I want to get enough money together so that we can get out. I can go legit in business and get away from drugs - I just need some cash to get started.

Devil   [*Narrows his eyes like - this one is tougher than usual… he whispers in Jack's ear again*]

Jack   I've got issues - don't think I don't know I've got issues. 'Course

I've got issues. I don't even know who my father is - I walk down the street every single day and look into the face of every man I meet of his age and I wonder "Could it be you - are you my Dad?" - and I can't even ask my Mum. My Mum isn't straight long enough in the day to even remember. She probably doesn't know. All she wants to do is drink. All she ever wanted to do was drink.

Devil *[Gives Jack an approving look like 'nice one - I've seen that played well, but that was outstanding' he gives the 'ok' hand sign]*

[silence – Jack is now sat with his back to the door as well]

Devil   [Shakes his head like – is she even in there – nobody withstands that? He nods his head repeatedly like – I'm going to my stash box now. He whispers to Jack]

Angel   [Moves across the bathroom to get Cara a glass of water and takes her hands off Cara's ears]

Jack   [*Jack opens his mouth like he has just realised exactly how to get the door open – he stifles his reaction and smiles. Knowing she can't see him he licks his lips before he delivers the killer line… knowing it is going to be <u>the</u> killer line.*]

The only person I ever relied on or trusted was me. I don't know how to love and I don't know how to trust. Anyone I ever tried to love *burned me* – and when I say they burned me… You remember those marks you saw on my body, on my arm and that? I told you those burns were self-harm. Those weren't self-harm Cara. *Those weren't self-harm.*

Cara   *[breaking her silence]* Oh Jack - I'm sorry

Jack   *[Knowing that he's got her]* Nah - It don't matter now. I've ruined this now too. Haven't I? I don't… You see… *[Gaining confidence now, he goes onto the front foot, he goes in for the kill]* We can't all have parents that live in fancy houses and drive fancy cars. You can get up and leave this shithole whenever you like Cara - go back to Bromsby and your big house and your massive bedroom. I ain't got that Cara. All I've got is me - and it's less than nothing *when I'm being honest with myself.*

Cara   Don't say that Jack

[Angel Looks stunned and mortified, heartbroken that Cara is being manipulated. The Devil looks at Jack like 'my work here is done' he nods in approval, before leaving the room. Exit the Devil]

Jack   You know that I can't stand the idea of you being with anyone else. How am I supposed to cope with that – how could you? How could you? What am I supposed to react like? Yeah – I got angry. I can't help what it provokes in me. You knew what I was when you got involved in me. You want all the rest of it. Well this is me Cara. You don't want me now, do you?

Cara   Don't talk like that… Look, I'm alright, I'm fine… it doesn't matter… I'll be out in a minute…

Jack   It does matter Cara - what you did - it does matter, that's my point… I can't be responsible for how I react to that. What you don't know is that you're the only person who has ever seen me for who I am. *You're the only one who gets me.* You're the only one who has ever shown me any love - for real. You're the only one who can make me better, who can change me and save me…

I *love* you Cara. I do.

I don't think your parents do. They're never around. Nobody ever sees them. It's all work, work, work. When are they ever there for you Cara? I think you need me just like I need you. We're two halves us two. We make one. As soon as we get school out of the way, we can get a place. Settle down - I'm already making enough money - you don't even need to work, I'll look after you. You don't need anybody else. *You've got this*. I'll be there for you…

Cara [*The bathroom door opens*] Jack come here - it all just got out of hand - you're right, I shouldn't have talked to Aiden. I don't know why I did that. I'm sorry - can you forgive me?

As they embrace Cara's phone begins to ring... she looks down at the screen and the name 'Sandford Oaks Care Home for the Eldery' is highlighted on the screen

Cara   Oh for god's sake, they've been ringing and ringing. Let me just see what they want, Jack

Hello?

Care Home   Hi, can I speak to Cara Walker please?

Cara   Yes? Speaking?

Care Home   Oh thank goodness – I've got hold of you. I've been trying to contact your parents. I'm not sure if I have their correct details on file…

Cara	This doesn't sound good at all – what… what has happened?

Care Home	Look – you're a minor, I shouldn't say… I just need to reach your parents.

Cara	What's happened to him?

Care Home	Can you please contact your parents and get them to call us as soon as possible?

Cara	Oh my god. He's gone, hasn't he? He has… he's gone… I can feel it…

Care Home	Look I… I really cannot say

Cara	When? Just tell me when!

Care I'm afraid your Grandfather passed
Home away two days ago. *(long pause)*
      There is a great urgency around this
      and we need to speak to the next of
      kin on behalf of the coroner. We are
      sincerely sorry for your loss, but
      can you please have one of your
      parents call us or come down
      Sandford Oaks as soon as is
      absolutely possible please?

Cara *[Numbly]* Yes. Of course. I'm so
      sorry. Thank you.

[Lights down. Scene closes.]

Act 3
Scene IV – *Death Threats*

Jack is dealing on the street when he is approached by two guys – older than him – that he knows works for the main county lines operator: Charlie and Brown. He nods at them knowingly and they beckon him over. He goes to them, and they sit him down next to them on the low wall. They fist bump.

Brown   Jack, you're doing well. We can see that you're doing well.

Jack   Smiles yeah – well, you know you have to hustle bit… *[brushing off his shoulders]*

Charlie slaps Jack hard to the face. The impact and the shock knocks Jack to the ground. He wasn't expecting it. It came out of nowhere. Rap beat comes in – dark 'gangsta rap' flavour with a West Coast inspired minor key.

[Song 12: Charlie & Brown's Rap]

Through the development of the song Jack is placed down on his knees, his knife is taken from him and Brown produces a Glock 9mm G43 pistol. This terrifies Jack.

Brown   *I like you Jack*

You're a good boy, innit?

I brought you up in this game

And I want you in it

You got talent

And you get things done -

Don't mistake my purpose

I don't want to put this on you son.

You know I'm on your side here,

I'm so sincere,

I'd take a bullet for you

Am I being clear?

> Like my baby brother
>
> I haven't got another
>
> But You called my boss 'a pussy'…

Big silence [shock]

Brown &   It's trouble Sunshine
Charlie
> The Boss said, Sunshine,
>
> It's time to find you,
>
> Leave you dead.
>
> So too bad Sunshine
>
> You are a dead man
>
> We're gonna put a bullet in your head

Jack   I swear to God I never did!

          [interjects]

Brown   Then why's he got it on his

          Instagram kid?

Charlie   Don't fuck with me –

          And don't deny it

          You'll make it ten times worse

          And You know you'll die for it

Brown   This is shit, I'm gonna end this big man

Do what we came to do here, while we still can

Tape up his mouth, and put him in the van

Leave him at the bottom of a river like a frogman

Jack   Now now mate we don't need to go there

Take a minute off –

We can get this sorted out – I swear

Brown	What the boss wants,
	the boss gets,
	That's your problem,
	Those are your regrets.
	I got my orders - so we got to hit it
	[to Charlie] Let's waste this mutha-f*cker
	In the next two minutes
Brown & Charlie	It's trouble Sunshine
	The Boss said, Sunshine,
	It's time to find you,
	Leave you dead.

So too bad Sunshine

You are a dead man

We're gonna put a bullet in your head

[Brown cocks the pistol to kill Jack, Jack hunches his shoulders expecting the shot at any moment now]

Charlie   Wait! [Pause]

I think I've got an idea –

Give me a minute here

There might be another way out

This could be his lucky year

Don't be austere with the fear

Or too ready with the sneer,

we can get him off the hook

We can get him in the clear

Jack   Yeah - we can sort this out…

Charlie   Calm down Jack - shh - it's ok son

You said what you said -

What's done is what's done

You're gonna get hurt - but we won't kill

Brown   Speak for yourself mate

Cos I fucking know I will

Charlie   Not gonna lie to you

I was losing sleep

Didn't want to come here and

I didn't want to speak

I couldn't get my head down,

What about you Brown?

Brown   I slept like a fucking baby, lets waste this clown

Charlie   Don't let him get you down… He's a psychopath,

He's on the war path

He's never happy 'til it ends in a bloodbath

He stabbed his own grandma for a fucking laugh

Then he denied it and he passed the fucking polygraph

Brown & Charlie
It's trouble Sunshine

The Boss said, Sunshine,

It's time to find you,

Leave you dead.

So too bad Sunshine

You are a dead man

We're gonna put a bullet in your head

Charlie   the boss likes the girl that he hangs with

Brown   Cara?

Charlie   Yeah, she's quite hot, and he'd like to have her

If Jack's sensible, I think he could offer

To put her in front of the boss dressed up proper

If she was cooperative, she could do us all a favour

Sit on his lap for a bit – she's a real lifesaver

And She'll come back tomorrow in the morning, yawnin'

Now you're off the hook, there's a new day dawnin'

Bros before hoes, she don't need to know

That you don't really love her,

We don't love them hoes [together]

What do you think Jack? You're not an idiot

Get yourself off the hook - but will she do it?

Can you trick this bitch? Can you make her switch?

If we can get her on the street she could make us rich!

Brown   If she refuses we can drug her…

Charlie Rohypnol, Valium, Ecstasy or Viagra

Both   It's trouble Sunshine

The Boss said, Sunshine,

It's time to find you,

Leave you dead.

So maybe Sunshine

You're not a dead man

But you'll have to put Cara in his bed

Musical interlude fades out

Jack   No no, I, I think she'll do it ok?

Charlie   Good lad Jack - now why don't you go and get her? Bring her back here for, what? About 6PM?

Brown   And don't you ever forget - you owe me a favour now, and I will stab you in the neck if you ever disrespect my boss again.

[Jack begins to hurry away]

Brown   Oh and Jack? [calls him back]

Jack   Yeah Brown?

Brown   [Sings to Jack acapella (Cold Play)] "Look at the stars! Look how they shine for you!"

[Shows Jack the middle finger] Fuck you Jack you little pussy [laughs]

[Jack exits]

Charlie   [Bursts out laughing] What a child! Did you see his face when you pulled that knife out? What a fraud! I'm telling you next time I get to be the psycho – you get all the fun!

Brown   What the boss wants, the boss gets! We better get back and tell him that he's having the girl…

[They exit together]

Act 4

Act 4
Scene I: *Cara's Bedroom II*

The scene opens with the Angel, Aiden and Cara in Cara's bedroom. Aiden is the only person who knows she is pregnant. Cara has called him over because she needs to talk to someone and she needs advice. She plays with the locket around her neck rubs her clavicle in anxiety whilst pacing around the room. The Angel is sat on the bed, listening quietly.

Cara   Aiden I'm sorry to drag you over here to talk about my problems. I don't really know where to begin…

Aiden   You have no idea how happy I am to talk to you again Cara.

Cara   Well I wish the circumstances were different…

Aiden   Don't worry – whatever the circumstances are we can face them together as… friends.

Cara   You really don't know what that means to me right now. I feel like I've got nobody.

The Angel   *Oh that's nice, a real kick in the teeth. So what am I? Chopped liver?* [Rolls her eyes]

Cara   Well I just don't know if I should keep this baby, or tell Jack… or…

Aiden Well I don't wanna say something out of turn – but I guess you called me over here for my advice, so I could be wrong but, here's how I see it Cara. I don't like Jack. You know I don't. But it's his baby too, and he deserves to know. Whatever you decide is what you decide – and no, he probably won't stick around – but he still deserves to know. I just don't think that you should let the circumstances make a dishonest person out of you…

Cara   But I'm scared Aiden. I really am. I'm scared.

Aiden   Look – the truth takes courage – but I'm always here for you. I'm not going anywhere. What do you think you could do that could push me away now? [he smiles gently]

Cara   I don't know but if you said two months ago I'd be drinking, doing drugs, having sex, and helping Jack to escape the police… [shakes her head] So who knows? I am so ashamed of myself. [she cries a little]

Aiden   Do you love him? Do you really love him?

Cara   Well… I…

There is a loud bang on the front door and Cara shouts

Cara   It's not a good time ok?

Jack   It's me! Cara – it's me! Let me in?!

Cara   Oh shit, it's Jack. [panicked] Aiden…I didn't lock the door!

They hear the door opening downstairs. Jack has let himself in. Panic spreads through Cara as she hears him coming up the stairs to her room in bounding strides.

Cara   Right get under the bed, I'll drop the blanket. No matter what happens, no matter what gets said – promise me, now promise me Aiden – you will

                    not come out of there until he's
                    gone

Aiden   I don't care if he finds me. I don't
        care.

Cara   Please Aiden, please! He's coming!
        Please!

Aiden looks at her – looks into her face – nods gently and gets under the bed. She drops the blanket over the edge of the bed to hide him, and he lays perfectly still barely taking a breath.

Jack   You're not gonna believe what I just
        found out today – and I swear – this
        is all *your* fault!

Cara   Jack I really need to tell you something…

Jack   I know. I found out and it's pretty awful isn't it?

Cara   *[Cara sits down on the bed slowly and begins to cry]* I just didn't know how you'd take the news when you found out.

Jack   How long have you known?

Cara   Well I don't know – what like a week?

Jack   How did *you* know so quickly? Why didn't you say? For god's sake Cara, this is a life!

Cara   I don't know I just…

Jack   Well look – I guess that doesn't matter now. I suppose it's a good thing that you know and I know now and *we both need to do something about this*. Get this sorted out.

Cara   *You want to get it sorted out?*

Jack   I mean – this is your fault really. I mean, we talked about this right, and *that* whole situation was on you.

Cara   Well – I mean – it kinda does take two…

Jack   Look - I know that I forgave you and everything and maybe I was a bit soft on you, but you know me Cara - *you manipulate me* and you get your way - but there's a price on me now and those guys are gonna kill me unless I come up with something pretty extraordinary.

Cara   Er… what are you talking about? *Why would they do that? Who?*

Jack   Er - well… you know - how dumb are you!? The incident with Aiden right? *The stuff I said?* Well somehow it got caught on camera and I'm gonna bet it was that little gay-boy Aiden snitching on me. *I mean, who else could it be?* What I can't get my head round is how he found out how to get that to the Boss – *how does he know him?* I have to hand it to the little shit – I didn't think he had it in him. Not gonna lie – but that's ok – I'm gonna settle him for that – you see if I don't. The next time I see him, I'm gonna stab him with this knife *[shows Cara a small pocket knife]*.

[Searching his person frantically] Where's my lighter, I need to smoke some weed to calm down. I need some weed *right now.*

Cara   Please don't smoke in here – my parents will smell it and I won't be able to see you for months. *[mentally trying to catch up]*

Jack   Do you want some?

Cara   No – please Jack – just, just wait until you're outside ok?

Jack   Why what's wrong with you?

Cara   I told you my parents will go ballistic!

Jack   Alright – ok – ok… ok…

Cara   I'm just trying to get my head around all this. They, they – you said *they* want to kill you and you think *Aiden* filmed you? I'm not sticking up for him Jack – I swear – but I saw him and he wasn't on his phone at all. He was on the floor the whole time. He never had his phone in his hand…

Jack   [*showing agitation*] Oh this again… you're gonna defend your little lover boy right? You gonna lie for him? Cara - you are so thick sometimes! I'm not lying! Thick! There was me, you and him. I'm not gonna snitch on *me* am I - so was it him or was it you? Was it you? Was it though?!

Cara   No of course it wasn't Jack you're talking crazy right now!

Jack   Nah - I'm talking *logic*. I know it wasn't you. I'm just doing the maths here for your little girlie brain. This is man business. Let me explain this one to you: If it wasn't *ME*, and it wasn't *YOU*, it was definitely HIM - do you understand?!

Cara   How can we be sure that there wasn't anyone else around? I mean, we were in the park Jack?

Jack   Do you need me to knock some sense back into you?! *I swear to God* - if you defend that tragic little sweetheart one more time - I know you've got a thing for him. Are you shagging him, Cara? TELL ME - are you two shagging?

Cara   God no Jack - no - not this again, please Jack no… *[Cara's eyes flick across to her bathroom door]*

Jack   [*Following her eyes. He calmly steps beyond her and between her and the bathroom.*] Not this time Cara. If you need some sense knocking into you, you're gonna get some sense knocking into you…

Cara   I'm sorry Jack – no – please – I'm sorry Jack, I'm so sorry. I swear.

Aiden starts to get restless beneath the bed and he's very close to coming out to defend Cara now. Cara can feel the subtle movements beneath her and she says loudly

Cara   No! It's ok – we got this… remember what you promised me! *You promised.*

Aiden listens to Cara and lays with a fist clenched beneath the bed

Jack   Promises promises Cara! I didn't know this shit was gonna get me killed! It's a bit different now isn't it? There's no unconditional promises in this world Princess! And this whole situation is on you. You know that! Imagine me - walking home - I was happy. I was bringing you some money home. I was gonna buy you something nice and pretty. All I was thinking about was how to make you happy. There you were - at it with the school loser in the middle of Sandford Park. If I'd been there *five minutes later* you'd been riding him right there.

[As Jack's temper escalates he picks up the picture that Cara has of Granddad at her bedside and he smashes it off the wall]

This is definitely not ok Cara! SO I lost it – who wouldn't?! Which bloke honestly *wouldn't?* Of course, I lost it – I wasn't thinking right at all – and that was because *you* knocked me right on my ear. After everything that I've done for you!

Jack *[Licks his lips and shakes his head]* If we're gonna sort this, you're gonna have to do something very different.

Cara What? What are you talking about Jack?

Jack   *[Growing calmer]* Well, Cara, it's like this actually. The Boss has offered a straight deal really and fortunately for us - we're kind of lucky right - because, you can actually make up for what you did wrong and how you brought this on. You just have to be… *nice to him*. You know? Like how you're nice to me? Sometimes?

Cara   *You want me to... what?*

Jack   You know - we just get that nice little dress on that you have, those nice heels that make you look so good… and then we'll go and see him… and all you have to do is help him to feel good. Flirt with him. Be nice to him. Have a good time with him. You'll be done in like an hour *tops* – maybe even sooner if he likes you. You've got this.

Cara   Wha *[voice cracking]* at?

Jack   This is not the time to be prissy Cara. You didn't think that I was gonna be the only man you ever slept with *right*? I'll just be the best. This isn't a fairy tale love. Most girls your age have had like six or seven blokes. A bit of experience won't hurt you – *you'll probably enjoy it a bit* – it will be over and done with and then we'll be in the clear…

Cara   I just don't know that I can Jack

Jack's phone alerts him to a message arrival. He checks it instinctively. It's from Aiden. It shows up on the back of the stage, reading: "I heard you were looking for me? Is everything ok. I'm at the park if you want to see me."

Jack   Look - Cara - I gotta go ok...

I love you Cara - we need this - and then we get out. Ok - I promise - this won't happen again. We'll add up what we've got and we'll get straight. Ok? We'll get this threat off us - and we'll call it a good ride that we had, and I'll get tidy. We'll leave all that drugs shit behind. Just you and me. I've had enough - I swear now. But I can't walk away while I owe this guy -

he's just not like that. You know that. This man's a vicious killer. When you get a visit off his boys you know they're real…

Cara… I… I… I'm scared. There is nobody else out there who can actually protect me from this now. They put it to me like that. If you love me… if you really love me… this is the time that you show me what that means. You know that I'd do anything for you Cara. If the shoe was on the other foot. You think I'd let someone come for you? *No way*. And usually that's how it is… when them girls were all on your back – who settled that beef?

Cara   It was you Jack

Jack   Damn right it was me! This is do or die Cara… do or die!

Cara   Ok - ok… you're right. It *was* my fault. I love you. I will do this. Ok. But look at the state of me! I need to get… to get ready I guess. Look - go home, give me half an hour - is that ok? I'll come over to yours…

Jack   Good girl Cara - I knew that you'd never let me down… half an hour yeah?

Jack exits. Cara falls to her knees. She is trying to regulate her breathing. She runs off stage and is sick. Aiden manages to get himself out from under the bed. Cara comes back on stage, wiping her mouth.

Aiden   You got rid of him? *[exhales]* Well done! Come on let's get you out of here. You can stay at mine. We'll tell your parents what has been going on. We can go to the police. We'll get this whole situation straightened out – *you are so lucky to escape that*

Cara   No. Aiden. I've gotta go. They're gonna *kill* him. I've seen these people Aiden. They're not joking. They'll kill him. All I have to do… it will take no time… and then… I've got to make sure that he's safe. *It was my fault.*

The Angel is sat with them and she is looking between the two faces. She's staring at Cara in desperate disbelief. She offers shocked facial expressions and open hands. He nods furiously when Aiden speaks.

Aiden   It wasn't your fault! You can talk to whoever you like in a park Cara! You never made him sell drugs for a gang! Please Cara - don't do this… I'm begging you. Come with me instead..

Cara kisses Aiden on the cheek. It's so gentle. She looks into his eyes. The Angel cries in a silent and earnest way.

[Stage lights go down. End of scene.]

Act 4
Scene II: *Sex & Death*

The scene opens with Cara hurrying towards the stage down the central aisle of the auditorium from the back. Cara is dressed as if she is going to a nightclub but doesn't know what she is going to be confronted by. She is terrified. A notification sound plays throughout the auditorium. Cara checks her phone. An overhead projection displays the contents of her phone screen. She has nineteen missed calls: a combination from Mum, Dad, and Aiden. She opens a voicemail from her Mum as she arrives on the stage.

Voicemail	You have one new message and zero saved messages. New message: [beeps]
Cara's Mum (voice)	Cara love - please pick up the phone.

I've been calling and calling you and I know that makes me sound like a hypocrite cause I don't always answer when you call me but I always ring you back in the end.

It's been days Cara. And we're worried. Really worried.

You've changed.

I know losing Granddad has been hard - it's been hard for all |

of us- but this started before that.

We barely see you anymore, I get calls from the school saying you're not in lessons, that your grades are dropping. You're dressing differently, you don't talk to us like you used to - you haven't for months, you're not eating, you're never in the house and when you are, you're always locked in your room.

You're not you anymore.

Look, are you in trouble? Because if you are, we can fix it together. It's okay, I promise. I won't be mad. Whatever it is, we'll find a way. Just call me back. Or text one of us. Just send us something to let us know you're okay.

Please.

I've cancelled my meetings for the next few days cause I know I've let work get in the way recently and I thought we could use some 'us' time. Just you and me. We could go shopping, watch a film...anything. Just come home. Your Dad is out looking for you right now - he's so worried, Cara. We love you so much. We just need to know you're okay. Please.

The message ends. Cara looks out to the audience in desperation. She realises then and there that she is truly trapped. She doesn't want this anymore. She wants to go home but she is in too deep now to escape whatever is about to happen. She turns to run down the central aisle and gets halfway down it before she meets Jack who appears from the door at the back of the auditorium. Cara stops dead. It's too late.

Jack   Hey, you made it… [taking her by the hand and practically dragging her up towards the stage.] come on, we're late

Cara   Jack…I…

Jack   You'll be fine - you look amazing, *you've got this Cara*

Cara   Stop! Stop! I'm sorry Jack I just don't think I can go through with this. I don't think I can do it… I feel sick…

Jack   Seriously? We talked about this! I know you don't want to do this babe - *but you're just taking responsibility for your own actions.*

Cara   Well.. I… [confused]

The Boss arrives, with Charlie, Brown and The Devil. The Boss is an intimidating

Godfather like figure. Jack tries to talk to him directly.

Jack   I just wanted to… *[before he can say 'apologise']*

The Boss shakes his head quietly and puts a finger to his lips to silence Jack immediately

Jack   But I…

The Boss shows the palm of his hand without eye contact.

Jack   Please…

Brown   I think he wants to apologise to you Boss…

Boss   [To Brown] I DON'T REMEMBER ASKING YOU A GOD-DAMN THING!

Brown looks embarrassed and drops his head. He is immediately submissive.

Boss   [Speaks to Charlie quietly] Tell him [Jack] that he is disrespecting me in front of the young lady. I didn't invite him to say a word. I don't want this to escalate.

Charlie   [Looks at Jack] When we want your opinion Jack, we'll give it to you.

Brown   Why don't you come with us? The Boss wants to get to know the young lady better.

Jack   [glances fearfully over at Cara who is looking more and more fearful] Er.. [he is guided away assertively by Charlie and Brown]

As Jack is walked away, Brown slips something over the knuckles of his right hand, and checks his shoulder to see that Cara is looking the other way, he punches Jack hard in the stomach and Jack doubles over before slowly going down to his knees trying to breathe. Charlie talks to him quietly saying "Shhh - It's ok, it's ok, you can breathe, take a deep breath" and *while he has Jack's full attention, Brown hits him over the back of the head with a blunt object which is handed to him by the devil who looks the other way. The blow renders Jack unconscious. Jack is knocked out laying at the back of the stage. Cara has seen nothing of this. [Exit Charlie and Brown]*

As the devil follows them, he takes out a knife and places it down on the stage in an apparently random spot which is strangely deliberate. [exit the devil]

The Boss   Now now, aren't you a pretty girl? *[chewing]* You've made a real effort haven't you?

The Boss gets into the intimate space of Cara, she gulps and leans backwards slightly, away from him, although her feet stay put as if fixed to the ground. Her body is rigid with anxiety. She is suppressing a panic attack and is only moments away from hyperventilating. The Boss runs the edge of his hand down the side of her face, from the temple down and with one finger along her jaw line before lifting her chin with the tip of his finger. It is a well-practised move.

The Boss   So very, very pretty. I do love pretty things.

He blows air into her face and she flinches slightly, her fringe lifted by his stale breath.

The Boss   It's ok Cara – that is your name, isn't it? Cara? Don't worry. This will make it better. Open up... *[he takes a single tablet out of his pocket and rubs the edge of it around her lips like a lipstick. He pops it into her mouth and smiles slightly]*

A tear escapes Cara's eye and she fights to stay in control.

The Boss   Swallow it. Swallow it. *Swallow it* *[Cara gulps]* there. You'll feel much better now... I know you want it.

He runs his hand Cara's side, from her under arm, to her midriff before moving in to kiss her neck, as a vampire might deliver a bite, and Cara gulps and tilts her head away exposing her neck. She looks up to the sky with her eyes and the silent tears runs down her face.

The Boss kisses Cara's neck and runs his hand across her waistline towards the middle - like a spider creeping across her midriff - it appears that his hand is on the way towards her groin - but it is moving slowing and with agonising tension.

Cara's face displays complete disgust, and the tears continue to run. It seems to take forever.

Aiden enters from the side of the stage, seeing what is happening. He sees the knife - left on the stage by the devil - and he picks it up impetuously. He sprints at the Boss, shouting at him

Aiden   GET YOUR HANDS OFF HER!

The Boss turns towards Aiden in confusion and anger.

Aiden plunges the knife deep into the upper arm of the Boss leaving it there. He steps backwards in his own shock.

Boss   Aaaagh! Bastard!! *[he clutches the wound and staggers to one side - he summons his henchmen]* CHARLIE! BROWN!

The Boss pulls the knife from his own arm and swings it wildly towards Aiden, but as he does so Cara leaps forward shouting "No!" and the knife slashes her deeply and viciously across the stomach in a single movement. The outfit that she is wearing shows her naked midriff and she clutches it with both hands turning away from the audience as blood spills with frightening volume. Sirens can already be heard in the distance. The strobe lighting frantically turns from red to blue, flickering wildly. The Boss looks at Aiden with furious direct eye contact.

The Boss   You are a dead man Aiden Ramsey!
               [Boss exits urgently]

Aiden runs over to Cara's side and cradles her in his arms as she lays her weight into him. They are both sobbing.

Aiden   Oh my God. Oh my god. I'm so sorry Cara – this is *my* fault – I shouldn't have ever let this happen. I should have protected you. [To himself] There's so much blood.

You're okay, just look at me. I'm here. God this is bad. I should've been there for you. I should've stopped this earlier. I should've run faster. I should've… I…

Cara   Shhhh it's okay [drowsy]

Cara reaches up and strokes Aiden gently on the cheek – she doesn't need words to respond. They share a tender, beautiful moment where neither speaks but everything is said. Whilst this is happening, the devil walks across to Jack. He slaps him on the face to bring him back to consciousness. As Jack comes around, the devil places a knife on the ground beside him. He walks away to the other side of the stage. As Jack is coming around, he feels blood at the back of his own head. Looking around, his eyes slowly clear and he sees Aiden and Cara intimately holding each other. As he looks across the devil rolls his eyes and makes a facial gesture like 'That's your girl bro'.

Jack sees the knife on ground beside him, he clutches at it, gets to his feet unsteadily, and lurches towards where Aiden is sitting.

Cara   I love you Aiden

Before Aiden can respond, Jack plunges the knife desperately into Aiden's back before staggering backwards off balance.

Cara   I think I always loved you really. I just didn't see it.

              NO! NO! WHAT DID YOU DO? WHAT DID YOU DO?? PLEASE NO PLEASE

>   NO! *[she holds Aiden's face in her two blood-stained hands]*

Cara then recognises in a second what has happened. She screams.

The devil smiles and walks off stage. Aiden's head drops into his chest his eyes fall closed.

In panic she makes it to her knees, covered in blood, her face is smeared… discovering the knife in Aiden's back. Aiden's lifeless body slumps into her. He is dead.

Jack, gulping for air is rugby tackled by a pair of police officers who suddenly arrive. He is dragged off stage in handcuffs following a scuffle.

An ambulance crew get to Cara, and she is taken away – hysterically screaming and trying to get back to Aiden. The Angel enters (dressed as a paramedic) and checks Aiden for signs of life. He gravely shakes his head and covers Aiden's upper body and head with a white sheet. As the police tape the crime scene, he begins to sweep away the debris – including a knife – not looking at the audience. As he gets to the edge of the stage he smirks at the audience and utters a single line:

The devil   "What the boss wants, [pause] the boss gets."

[Exit the devil]

Act 4

Scene III: *Hospital*

Cara is in hospital – it is not clear whether this is an A&E ward, whether it is general admissions or a psychiatric unit, but it is clearly a hospital ward for children. The walls are decorated with badly painted pictures of giraffes and elephants. There are pictures and finger paintings on the walls, and it highlights an expectation of children that seems strangely at odds with Cara – 15 years old, sat firmly upright and ostensibly alone, staring blankly out into the audience – numb and frozen in shock and trauma. In the bed beside Cara's is a familiar child – a younger child – with a distinctive jacket draped on the back of a chair. A traumatised parent sits with a tear-stained face. The child is 'Junior'. He is breathing only with the help of a ventilator, and he looks incredibly fragile and small. Mum keeps crossing herself and repeatedly clutches her rosary beads.

Cara remains motionless whilst a recording of Aiden's last voicemail plays throughout the theatre. It's the voicemail she never got to hear and now she's listening to it, injured and empty, all too late.

Voicemail	You have one new message and zero saved messages. New message [beeps]
Aiden	Cara… it's Aiden. Are you safe? God, please tell me you're safe. I can't let you go through with this. I'm so worried about you. Look, I know you feel like you owe Jack and like somehow this is all your fault, but it's messed up. This whole thing is so twisted. You never deserved this – not any of this and I can't stand by and watch you get used again and again by them. You are worth so much more, I swear.

I'm coming to get you Cara. Don't you worry. I'm going to come and get you and I'm going to take you away, far away from here. Away from all this. You'll see. Just hang on…

I… [he pauses] I love you

But I think you've probably always known that.

The message ends with a harsh beep. A single tear runs down Cara's cheek. She remains completely motionless. Out of her earshot, two doctors are in consultation. One is strangely familiar to us – The Devil – and he is instructing a Junior Doctor:

The Devil Look at the state of this one eh? Another one. [flicks the page of the chart over] So predictable. Another knife trauma. Lucky to be here. Probably doesn't deserve it – let's not lie. I'm not saying all young people are like that – but you can tell the bad ones a mile away. If that was my daughter…

Anyway… knife trauma, mid abdomen, deep laceration, heavy bleeding, substantial blood loss – transfused upon arrival – pain relief, now on morphine – will need to be watched carefully with that. Unknown history of drug abuse – probable dependency issues – certainly *was* pregnant, first trimester, consequential miscarriage – saved the social services a bloody fortune that did – am I right? I really don't think she's ever going to carry to term after this to be honest. That's her lot – but it's not a worry for us at this stage of the game. [flicks page impatiently] twenty-seven stitches across, lucky not to sustain intestinal injury really. Nil by mouth until we can actually make sure that the intestine is completely intact – but we're 99% sure at this point. Unexplained haematoma to the back of the head and parts of the body - seem to be from a different incident - are gradually healing. Someone has tried to knock a bit of sense into her but I bet it wasn't her parents… bruising to the neck looks like a love bite - nothing more than that. Dirty cow.

Ok I'm satisfied that she is in a stable condition - her health is improving - I don't want her here too long, and I'll review her again in what? It's Friday now - I want to get on that golf course this weekend at some point - so let's call it 72 hours. [Mimie his golf swing]

Keep an eye on her but don't call me unless it's bloody necessary, ok?

Junior Doctor   Yes Sir… [writing down notes]

The Devil   Oh look at this bloke – I love this guy – turn this up… [pointing to the TV] this guy's brilliant, he's bloody brilliant. Such a good looking sod as well..

The local news is on and 'Look Westshire' is broadcasting news about a violent incident in Sandford Park. The local news reporter is relaying his version of the events. It is none other than the Devil himself, now in the mainstream news…

The Devil   You join me at Sandford Park, and what was designed to be a lovely and innocent playground for local infants was ruined today by tragic events. A brave local businessman appears to have been passing through the area on foot when he was accosted by rival gangs at around 6PM. As the daylight was fading, it has been said that one young hooligan tried to rob the affluent community leader – stabbing him without warning in the right arm with a knife. As this brave victim of crime wrestled with his own injury, a second male – thought to be from a rival gang – intervened. Now what is not clear is how a teenage girl was then hospitalised with a severe injury to her stomach. Medical authorities cannot comment and at this time the police are not releasing details of the event. What we do know is that one of the males – it would seem a violent and known criminal actively involved in the local underground scene - was left on the ground to bleed to death. One male is in police custody. Local sources are describing this as a potential robbery that went horribly wrong – and as a consequence of an inevitable turf war that has been brewing for some time. What is very clear to this reporter is that knife crime is becoming harder and harder to ignore in this area – and this is the second juvenile that has been hospitalised in recent days. I spoke to local Councillor, Terry Wood, who represents Sandford West, and he had this to say:

[Song 13: 'It's not my fault]

A range of adult professionals sing a verse each about why this situation is not their fault or of their making. Each takes their turn to wash their hands of this, blame each other and distance themselves from what has happened. The song highlights the collective failure of everyone.

As the song is performed Junior goes into a 'crash' situation and dies in the background as doctors and nurses work with futility to save him.

Junior Doctor   Heart rate plummeting – can I get some help here?! Resus!

As the song ends, Junior flatlines. He's dead. Tears trickle down Cara's face. She is traumatised and feels trapped in her own scarred body. She continues to sit, completely still, staring at the audience. The stage is loud and chaotic and she can't escape. As the stage lights go completely dark, the voice of Granddad is heard over the loud-speakers:

Granddad   It's OK Cara you can stop now – this is too painful – you've shared enough. Stop now.

Act 4
Scene IV: *Finale*

As the stage lights come back up, we are back in the support circle. Cara is looking at the Young Person's Worker in a state of confusion, as if she has been roused from a night terror. Cara is physically drained and looks like she could collapse at any time.

Young Persons Worker   It's ok Cara you can stop now – this is too painful Cara – you can stop now, you've shared enough, you don't have to keep going. You don't have to tell us any more. You're in a safe space now Cara - you're okay, it's going to be okay

Cara continues to stare blankly out at the Young Person's Worker as if she is a passenger in her own damaged body. The Young Person's Worker continues to de-escalate Cara and bring her back into the room, rubbing her hand and talking to her in soothing and reassuring tones. The people in the support circle all look bereaved - they have been crying. The atmosphere is sombre and impossibly futile. No one moves.

Cara   [wipes her eyes with the back of her sleeve] I'm sorry. I'm sorry. I'm so, so sorry. [sniffs] They're all dead and it's all my fault. Aiden, my baby - and

                    Granddad...he was totally
                    alone...I promised him...

Young   Cara you're a victim – this
Persons   wasn't your fault…
Worker

Cara   Maybe I deserve it. I don't know.
                Maybe this is some sort of sick
                punishment or something…

[Song 14: Cara's Regret – Solo]

There is a pervasive silence in the group. Dani rubs her thumb down the side of her nose and sniffs heavily.

Dani   I think I want to go next

Dani swaps places with Cara so that she is sitting in the centre of the stage.

Young Persons Worker   Well… ok Dani… go ahead [nodding]

DANI   I just want to say, before I start, that I wasn't always like 'this'. So please don't judge me for that…

[The stage falls dark]

The Devil walks through the auditorium to the stage. His pace is leisurely. He is peeling an apple with a knife, and he speaks in an even and dispassionate way.

The Devil And it goes round and round and round again. The same stories, different people. I mean none of this has to happen.

Eli, Junior, Dani, Jack, Aiden… Cara – all this could have been avoided. *'Could'* being the important word here because, really, it *could* have been. (Smiles) But it wasn't.

You know. It makes me wonder, whether I was even there. Whether I was even real. Whether this whole time, I was anything more than a mirage, a myth, a moment of madness inside their minds. Inside your minds.

How can you malign me? What? Did I make them do something they weren't going to do anyway? Or say something they wouldn't eventually say?

The Slanderer. The Deceiver. The Tempter. The Father of Lies. The Enemy. The Evil One...[pause] The *Devil* [smirks]: all names I've been called. But the truth is, names mean nothing, and their names will mean *nothing*.

Are they a story - or just a statistic? Something to shake your head at? No-one will ever sit these kids down and say to them that their lives were worth more than what they got. Instead, we'll all blame them and tell them that they deserved it. *Don't you think they deserved it?*

I say this again: names mean nothing. When you think about it - don't we all get to be our own devil? Don't we all make this world into our own personal hell?

And me? Ask yourself - was I even real? Or am I just your scapegoat? Am I just the worst parts of you packaged into someone fictional so that you can forgive yourself? Am I just something you created so that you have someone to blame for what happened here? Someone to blame, for **THE EVIL THAT WE DO.**

THE END.

Appendix A: Song List

Act 1
Opening number
Acapella Rap
Jack's Song
Granddad and Cara's Duet
Cara's Conflict

Act 2
Jack's Party Rap
Acapella Hangover Rap (Reprise of Acapella Rap)
Dani's Song
Aiden's Song

Act 3
Angel's Song
Confidence (Reprise of Granddad and Cara's duet)
Charlie & Brown's Rap

Act 4
Not My Fault
Cara's Regret

For the full musical scores, sheet music and resources to support your musical production please visit:

https://inclusive-development.co.uk/the-evil-that-we-do

Appendix B: Guidance for Schools on Content Moderation & Technical Staging –

Act 1

Scene 1 - A Church Yard

This scene presents two identified challenges - the first regards the beating up of a juvenile on stage by three gang members. This is naturally something that is going to potentially cause some distress and is definitely intended to grab audience attention right from the outset. Balancing the graphic nature of such an incident against the need to protect the audience is important.

In the original writing of this scene we envisioned that the character of Eli would be quickly taken to the ground within the first two blows that he receives. His character is to be hidden behind stage furniture in the church yard and as the audience see blows (punches and kicks) being delivered, they won't see them impacting on Eli. There will be a moment of distress when Eli is dragged from the stage to the wings - noises will allow the audience to fill in the details - but his robbery and whatever happens there is hidden from view.
If you are staging this in a school or a youth centre or for a predominantly young audience this has been written in such a way as to afford your direction some degree of discretion over how graphic this confrontation needs to be. In an educational setting we would recommend that you

document your thoughts and feelings on this matter - including what you choose to include and what you choose to leave out - and why.

A further point that might cause contention is that Eli urinates himself in the course of the incident. Looking at the psychology of this character - he is a young man, closer to childhood than adulthood actually - and he has never been in such a confrontation before. The transaction is turning into a traumatic nightmare - the kind of thing he has been warned about - and the worst possible outcome. In these circumstances people do lose bladder control and it is not uncommon for victims of robberies to soil or urinate themselves as a consequence of their natural bodily responses.

You may or may not want to include this, but it is a point of realism.

To convey what is happening the original production of this play has Eli dressed in lighter coloured trousers as dark trousers will not show the effect we are seeking to convey. The actor playing Eli has an artificial bladder constructed from an unobtrusive soft drinks bottle, with a modest amount of water, and a valve that can allow that water to pour from the approximate relevant area of his body causing a certain visual effect. *Contact us if you would like to know how we achieved this.* Again - as with any points of this play - if you find the point of action is likely to become an emotional trigger, we would advise your director to create a decision log on what will be retained and what will be removed, and if the play is being delivered in a school or youth setting, that decision log can be reviewed in consultation with the senior management of that institution or facility prior to a final decision being agreed.

Scene 2 - Support Group

Support Group is clearly another scene that could trigger memories and recollections of a variety of circumstances for different people. The setting of the support group doesn't last long and a production challenge will be fading it fairly rapidly into a classroom setting as the scene continues (this is a reflection of the fact that Cara then becomes our narrator, albeit with an omniscient retrospective).

In this scene Eli makes reference to the fact that he was also sexually abused while he was being robbed. You might think that this is a gratuitous point that has no place in the play (and indeed this is a point that you might wish to retain or edit this in your production) - however this is again a point of reality. Phil Priestley was a Detective Sergeant for 9 years and in creating the events around Eli he has incorporated facts of a true case (victim's name has been changed) [R v Hudson (2007) - Cambridge Crown Court] that Phil was involved investigating and prosecuting. The purpose of the detail is to underline the absolute vulnerability and uncertainty that accompanies any such transaction. This being said the writers acknowledge that this point - even in passing - could be upsetting for several members of the audience and directorial discretion is something that you might wish to consider here.

Scene 5 - Toxic Masculinity

While it isn't anticipated that this scene will be a particular trigger towards trauma there is a use of language and behaviour which is a sad reflection of a mainstream cultural attitude across a wide cross section of young men throughout their teenage years. The contrast between the things the characters say to each other - versus the reality of what the character 'Jack' sends in messages to Cara is important.

What we tend to know about toxic masculinity in the teenage cohort is that a large number of the young men perpetrating these qualities *(which clearly do have a significant negative impact on the overall quality of life for each other and for young women around them)* are very different around other people - such as parents, teachers, people in positions of authority, and their girlfriends (specifically when they are on their own).

We know that for the vast majority of young men (who display such behaviours) toxic masculinity is a posture, it is an adopted state of being, and it is a dishonest representation of their actual thoughts and feelings. By putting it on a stage we are giving young men who are watching this play (specifically) time to reflect and recognise where they have been guilty of the same or similar behaviours. What we are trying to do is create this with sincerity and in such a way that it can be recognised for this purpose - this leads us to using language that generates a generalised warning as it may offend.

Act 2

Scene 1 - The Party

'The Party' is a scene that encompasses a number of problematic teenage behaviours - including toxicity, drug experimentation, sexual promiscuity, peer pressure, and the threatening issue of drink spiking. The culmination of the scene has a sexual assault/rape incident through intoxication.

In the course of the party a toxic drink is passed around. Both Dani and Cara are drugged in this scene and the administration of those drugs (while all drug abuse is ill advised) is such that it raises issues and questions around consent and coercive behaviour.

Cara's consumption of an MDMA tablet is done in such a way as to demonstrate how Jack will not accept her boundaries and does not work within the parameters of her consent or permission. This is an unhealthy and abusive relationship - and this is what an unhealthy and abusive relationship looks like. It is not about a black and white relationship where a person is always 'mean' or 'nasty' towards their partner - they compromise their partner through emotional, psychological, sexual and physical abuses that manipulate on many different levels.

Victims often talk about how they couldn't defend themselves on so many levels - or feared not accepting the more 'seductive' version of a boundary compromise for fear of the violent or angry consequences and being forced anyway. Cara's drugging is an essential part of her character changing through the play and the transition that she makes from the beginning of the scene - where she is refusing alcohol. The situations and the risks subsequently become more acceptable to her – she acclimatises to unexpected things. It is also an important part of the immediate disinhibition of Cara because she becomes a character that she would not otherwise transition towards with such plausible speed.

The drugging of Dani is performed in a different way. It is done without identifying a specific perpetrator. The rational explanation for the 'devil' character is that he doesn't really exist - he is an elemental part of every character within the play - but we separate 'him' off to depersonalise and forgive our worse characteristics.

So we don't know *who* drugged Dani and how premeditated it was - we have diluted the element of targeting a specific character because that is a horrific crime to use as an incidental 'side' event. We have created it as a quasi-accidental event instead - something that the boys later 'take advantage of' in the worst way (they rape Dani - but the drug allows them to say, to themselves as much as anyone else, that she was responsible for her own intoxication and she consented 'really').

Dani is a rape victim, and hints at the fact that she has been raped before. She has had non-consensual sexual encounters and she doesn't know who with, how or where. This is helping to reframe in the mind of the audience exactly why this is so very wrong. This is not 'getting laid at a party when we were wasted'.

The aspect of having one drink subject to a spiking and passing it through the party is designed in such a way to create narrative tension. The aspect of Dani's rape is combined with the toxic quality of 'slut shaming' (scene 2) as the boys subsequently blame Dani for compromising *them* through *her* promiscuous behaviour (gaslighting). Comment is then passed that nobody would ever offer her fidelity or emotional intimacy as a consequence of that value judgement.

Consequently the party is full of details that are problematic, challenging and emotionally confrontational for the audience. We find them to be essential to the narrative and the overall purpose of the play and we don't feel that they can be removed without losing the artistic integrity of the staging.

This being said a particular action within the events is written as Jon wrapping himself and Dani (now drugged) beneath a blanket so that he can abuse her lack of resistance and free agency - while not demonstrating exactly what is happening to the audience. This could be softened by having Jon remove Dani from the stage altogether and by taking it completely out of the eyes of the audience. This will depend on directorial discretion and a careful evaluation of who you are staging your production for.

Scene 2 - The Hangover

The rape of Dani is explored in more detail in scene 2 as this event bridges between both scenes in a very important way - the characters are not sober in one scene, but they are sober (if hungover and potentially 'under the influence') in the next. Scene 2 presents the hindsight moralisation of immoral and illegal behaviour (rape). This is how toxic masculinity operates as a comfort blanket to young men who really know that they are up to no good. Indeed the phrase 'up to no good' is one that they might enjoy and celebrate as it softens and minimises 'rape' specifically with a 'boys will be boys' coverall and an inherent message of victim blaming (if you go to such a party you need to keep your wits about you and be on your guard etc etc).

Again this is an essential part of the play that we feel cannot be dispensed with as it covers a hostile landscape of risk and abuse.

Dani is revealed to be a lesbian in her solo song which is designed to take her from being a two dimensional victim character to someone who is relatable, more dynamic, and gives insight to her thoughts, feelings and aspirations. She is a real person with human rights, and, of course, an inherent human value that we all possess. We are inviting the audience to recognise that.

The fact that she is intended to highlight two important things: firstly that this toxic masculine landscape is heteronormative and suppresses individuality and the right to be yourself in a way that is incredibly important. The second point addresses consent - while it is very clear that Dani has been drug raped and did not and could not consent the writers are making a further point *very clearly*: even if Dani was sober she would not have sought a consensual sexual encounter with Jon because she is not heterosexual.

Scene 5 - Jack Ass

This scene is about Jack's increasingly wayward and risk taking behaviours. It shows the increasing compromises that Cara is making with her own moral perspective as she is now an active part of Jack's activities on the street. She is no longer someone who is external to it - she is participating.

Jack is seen to coach and mentor another, younger character - Junior - who becomes very relevant in the climax of the play. This is demonstrative of how street hierarchies work and how young people are beguiled into this lifestyle.

While all of the main characters in the play are young, Junior is even younger. He is barely out of primary school. The youngest criminally exploited child drug dealer that has been identified by the authorities in England and Wales is an 8 year old boy. This is a sad reflection of how this criminal underworld proliferates and expands.

Your staging and portrayal of Junior is (again) an important part of the narrative - it is not incidental or gratuitous - but how you frame his character is discretionary. We suggest that Junior wears a distinctive jacket because this will be needed in the hospital scene so that the audience know that it is Junior that dies. His death is portrayed in a more incidental way - as a piece of human collateral - we never tell the audience explicitly how he ended up in hospital (mention is made of 'another stabbing' when the news presenter reports later on) or what happened to him. What is essential for dramatic purposes is that the audience know

- at the conclusion of the play - that his tragic demise was an unexplored subplot and an aside to the events we have chosen to explore. This is one device that we have used to 'surround' the audience with the complexity and the prolific nature of these problems. Too many to look at or confront.

Scene 5 - Granddad II

This is likely to be a triggering and upsetting scene for some - particularly if anyone has recently lost a loved one under any circumstances whatsoever (and that would include COVID-19 where they were absolutely unable to visit their loved one through no fault or neglect of their own).

In the first 'Granddad' scene he is portrayed as an idyllic and loving figure of unconditional positive regard towards Cara. He is the only source of this in her life and he is actually the only character in the play - perhaps aside from Aiden - that she knows that she can get this from and who will always be there for her. In our original scene with Granddad, Cara promised Granddad that he would never be alone. This scene is a betrayal scene - because he is alone and more to the point, when Cara refuses to answer the call from the care home, he is killed as a consequence of that neglect.

While this is portrayed as a literal murder - it is an allegorical sequence to explain the way in which a person who is left in a state of isolation and decline is likely to give up on life.

The Devil character is disguised as a doctor - which introduces an abuse of trust issue and hints at circumstances where people in positions of power can let you down in a critical way. The Devil - throughout the play - adopts many forms, uniforms and disguises and the overarching purpose of this is to integrate and conceal him (primarily) but it also expresses how 'the Devil' (as a symbol of our failure and worst qualities as humans) lurks within all of us and the best of us.

The knife is used to create dramatic tension in this scene because we lead the audience to believe that Granddad is going to be killed in a violent and graphic way. Tickling the victim with a knife is a metaphor for everything that happens within the play of course - behind every action and outcome is the fear of violence and brutality - but more often than not the worst of it is delivered by other means and the violence and brutality simply reinforces the fear that makes such coercive and controlling behaviours possible.

Granddad is a symbol of Cara's innocence and her moral wellbeing. The death of Granddad clearly speaks to the decline in Cara's innocence, her losing her way, and leaving her childhood behind. Granddad and Aiden have a symbiotic relationship in so much as they stand for the same values and qualities - and if Aiden knew that Granddad existed you could plausibly imagine that he would have visited Granddad with Cara. When Granddad dies, Aiden becomes the moral guide light in her life. Anything within the staging that can help to express this would be in step with the intentions of the authors.

In the staging of Granddad's death, two combined suggestions are offered for consideration: First of all, the entrance of the Devil coincides with the background music of (perhaps muffled) drum and bass or dubstep music that allows foreboding bass that has the scooped out absence of midrange delivering a certain sense of emptiness. This music is alien to Granddad and it is an invasion of his privacy and comfort - it would be a horrible thing for him to die listening to (the antithesis of his preferences). The second aspect involves the use of strobe lighting (where available) for the moments where his breathing is smothered to create both a dramatic effect and to hint at a 'nightclub' type aesthetic to what is already a subverted environment. The use of any strobe lighting would need to be risk assessed and advertised at the outset of the play to give forewarning to any photosensitive epilepsy sufferers.

Act 3

Scene 1 - Pregnant

Unplanned pregnancy is at the heart of this sobering and alienating scene. Cara is beginning to encounter negative life outcomes. Within this scene we clearly suggest that Cara knew that even if she loved Jack, Jack would never love her back unconditionally.

Statistically it is almost a certainty that there will be women and girls in your audience who have experienced this scene for real in their own lives and they were confronted with the very real issues and considerations that an unplanned pregnancy brings.

The presence of the Angel is symbolic of the fact that people in such circumstances can lock themselves away (in their own mental 'bathroom') and convince themselves that they are alone. There are specialist support services and we emphasise the need to produce supporting materials and to advertise such materials for your audience in a way that you feel is appropriate. An example might be a table at the point of entry and exit that offers leaflets on a host of services and topics covered within the play.

We also ask you to consider the use of an impact room - if such a thing is available to you - where a person with relevant experience, expertise and empathy can speak to anyone who feels the need to leave the theatre due to any distress or anxiety they have experienced.

Scene 2 - Confidence

This scene is about contrasting a genuine dialogue between people (Cara and Aiden) who offer each other emotional sincerity against the version of 'love' that Cara has known with Jack.

There is a language warning for the entrance of Jack in the later part of the scene - but generosity in censorship has been given to the character here because his anger and his rage are not conveyed effectively otherwise.

Scene 3 - Coercive Control

This is a domestic abuse scene and within this scene there are huge issues of contention that are likely to cause distress and anxiety. Domestic abuse is far more prevalent than most people realise across all sections of society and all communities. It is reasonable to expect that one in three women within the audience will have been involved in an abusive relationship.

The scenario of a female having to flee to the bathroom (usually the only lockable room in the house) is commonplace and is likely to provoke a reaction.

In this scene Jack moves through a series of adopted and manipulative positions to regain coercive control over Cara. When he cannot physically beat or assault her any more, he becomes emotionally and psychologically abusive. It is important to understand that even through the locked door, Cara is still being harmed by Jack. She is not safe. The door is an illusion of safety - and this is how people live in abusive situations.

Jack fabricates different lines of approach to Cara and the Angel (unbeknownst to Cara) shields her ears from this abusive language. The language is beguiling, but it is still abusive.

We are highlighting all the aspects of gaslighting, blame attributing, straw-man arguments, grandstanding, the use of self-pity and guilt - all of the common manipulative tools of a domestic abuser. These are used knowingly and deliberately (not only by Jack but by the vast majority of all abuse perpetrators).

This language reaches a peak when Jack uses his self-harm injuries as a method of eliciting the control that he needs. Cara is an empathetic and compassionate person. He knows this - he tells her (falsely) that his self-harm injuries were inflicted by his parents. *This is structurally important* - it tells us that Jack doesn't understand his role as a victim (even under self-harm) or that the abuse he suffered and the outcomes of his struggle to cope, were not his fault. This hints at the intergenerational nature of abuse and the fact that there is a relationship between early life trauma and abusive tendencies (towards self and others) in later life. It also shows that Jack will lie and mislead about *anything* - anything at all - if it helps him to get his way. Contrast this with Aiden who is an honest character who lies about nothing and later advises Cara not to allow her personal circumstances to make her into a dishonest person.

Naturally the referencing of self-harm will have the potential to provoke or trigger a reaction and the portrayal of the self-harm (however it might be presented) is something that needs careful directorial consideration.

Scene 4 - Death Threats

This is probably the most problematic scene for many viewers, for schools and for community groups to contemplate. This is for a very important reason.

This scene marks the arrival of 'Charlie' and 'Brown' - not the 'rough around the edges' lads that they are potentially seen as (despite the robbery and the abuse of Eli at the outset of the play). They are not named after the 'Peanuts' character 'Charlie Brown' - they are named after the street names for cocaine (charlie) and heroin (brown). These are the products (alongside cannabis) that they commonly supply.

Charlie and Brown need to transfix the audience with just how amoral and nasty they actually are - we want the audience to be absolutely convinced that these out of town thugs will do anything that they are ordered to do. This includes murder. *They escalate everything.* Jack is taught to carry a knife - but they carry guns. They are older. They are more violent. They have no concerns at all about violence and their language is far more abusive and aggressive.

This is a true reflection of what County Lines handlers behave like. This is not gratuitous on any level.

The staged build up to the 'execution' of Jack - which is aborted only at the final minute in a set piece that the two main characters have repeatedly inflicted on others, is a piece of psychological abuse designed to ensure that that Jack would never step out of line for fear of his life. It is also designed to take possession of Cara and to drag her closer into the gang so that they can profit from her sexual exploitation.

This is what is at the heart of this form of organised criminality and it is absolutely at the heart of the play. It is horrible, it is traumatic and the deliberate purpose of this very dark scene is to take the audience up to the edge of their tolerance, within any reasonable permissions and boundaries.

For this reason the level of threat and language is way beyond what would be commonly anticipated in a production from a school or youth group and the 'shock value' of the piece is intended to leave a lasting effect while it takes and holds the attention.

Directorial discretion will be needed - but we urge production to retain the courage needed for the overall purpose of this play.

Act 4

Scene 1 - Cara's Bedroom II

This is another domestic abuse scene and shows the way in which domestic abusive practises are both learned and escalating in nature. Jack is again violent in his behaviour towards Cara, and in this scene he breaks a picture of Granddad - which of course is a symbolic piece of drama (showing how he broke that relationship and had a hand in the death of Granddad by coming between them).

They speak at cross purposes with separate concerns - but it is the concerns that Jack has for his own wellbeing that predominate and of course takes the agenda.

We also underline how cannabis becomes a dependency drug and how Jack cannot effectively self-manage his own anxiety or distress without the drug. Again, references to drugs within this passage are not gratuitous or frivolous or purely stylistic. We know that teenage drug abuse inhibits the development of the frontal lobe of the brain, and it leaves adolescent users with a deficit of emotional coping skills.

Cara's actions in this scene show that even someone that you might expect to behave in a more rational way (i.e. not offer herself to an organised crime boss to pay for an offence she never committed) can be conditioned through repetition, reinforced with mistreatment and emotional abuse. Cara genuinely feels indebted, and duty bound. Again, this could be a trigger point for some.

Scene 2 - Sex and Death

This is the most violent scene in the play - and while that will trouble some viewers - given the context of the psychological, sexual and emotional abuses that we've already witnessed (some under the threat of being visited with physical violence) the events of this scene are not beyond the tone that has already been set - *provided the balance struck by the direction and production have been carried out successfully.*

In this scene Jack is knocked unconscious in a swift and deliberate attack.

The Boss asserts himself as the apex predator by belittling Brown who terrified everyone in Act 3 Scene 4.

Cara is sexually assaulted and - once again - she is drugged. The actions of the Boss are chillingly deliberate and are performed slowly for the purpose of building and sustaining tension. *The actual hand movements of the Boss need to avoid intimacy, however, and the breasts, buttocks and groin are avoided.* The timed arrival of Aiden needs to be carefully choreographed to avoid the actual need for the Boss' hand to go below Cara's waistline.

Cara's midriff needs to be on display for theatrical purposes. On one level the Boss puts his hand on it and we wish to avoid him going beneath clothing. Additionally, when she is wounded we do wish to display that wound - noting of course that how this is done could be an impactive emotional event for the audience.

The arrival of Aiden is an uncharacteristic but violent one - as he plunges a knife (left by the Devil) into the Boss' arm. This is not enough to save Cara though and as the Boss removes the knife to use it against Aiden in retribution, Cara's intervention leads to her receiving a very serious stomach wound, blood loss and miscarriage.

The sound of sirens and the use of blue flashing lights in the distance give reason for the Boss to flee the scene without further violence - issuing threats to Aiden as he leaves (such as using his full name, the only time this is done in the whole play, nobody knows this information so how does the Boss know? This is part of the intimidation and threat of his character).

The events that then unfold - with a drugged and seriously injured Cara in the arms of Aiden. The audience might now anticipate that Cara is going to die in Aiden's arms - but the twist of the scene is delivered by Jack who murders Aiden and it is Cara that is left as the survivor.

How graphic these injuries and assaults are will be left to the director to consider in light of her or his props, audience, and the boundaries of what can be reasonably permitted in her or his or school/theatre setting.

Scene 3 - Hospital

This scene will need to be dressed as a ward for children - but the exact nature of that ward is deliberately unclear. Accident and Emergency? ICU? Psych? The presence of a dying child sustained on breathing apparatus in the bed next to Cara suggests the former as opposed to the latter.

Although the actions and events in this scene are not as graphic, the tone and the nature of the dialogue is provocative and undoubtedly the passing of a child will upset many. The Devil Doctor is judgemental and unsympathetic to Cara - and this is designed to provoke or trigger anger and antipathy towards him, and collective sympathy towards Cara.

The song piece in this scene will involve several professionals from different agencies explaining their lack of involvement and why they are not to be blamed. These individuals are self-concerned and not focused on the child dying behind them in crash resus. This will be impactive and problematic for some. It is, however, literally a conclusion of this play. We are showing that environments that host this form of criminality exist because the people who have the power to create supportive and nurturing communities for children and young people, have failed to cooperate or recognise their urgent responsibility.

Scene 4 - Finale

This is the literal finale of the play and it takes us back into the care/support circle that we began with. Circular imagery is very important to the play and we are destined to repeat Cara's traumatic journey with the equally traumatic telling of Dani's own journey. The same cautionary notes are applied to the presentation of the support circle environment.

The transition back into the circle is done in such a way as to highlight aspects of PTSD and we realise that actually as much as this is a telling from Cara, she is no longer in control of it - it's not a recollection, it is the reliving of trauma, it is a flashback. Any directorial support towards this impression is encouraged by the authors.

We need to acknowledge that simply moving into this ground is a potentially trigger event for some audience members. Again - support and signposting around PTSD and mental health at the end of the play is definitely advised.

About the Authors:

Natalia Huckle

This is the debut publication of this gifted and talented young writer of drama, prose and poetry. Natalia, at 17 years of age, has finished her GCSE exams and is currently on a gap year between GCSEs and A levels (which she will be studying in Cambridge).

Natalia's writing covers a broad spectrum of topics and concerns and her fiction is distinctive in its witty and intelligent dialogue, its strong characterisation, and a sincere feeling for how her protagonists interact with each other.

Thematically Natalia is a brave writer who wants to address the issues and concerns of her generation and is willing to confront the challenge of presenting sometimes harsh didactic and taboo messages to young audiences.

Natalia cites writers including Russell T Davies, Phoebe Waller Bridge, Margaret Atwood and Alan Bennett as inspiring figures in literature and script writing specifically.

Phil Priestley

Phil has previously written and published two non-fictional titles on the subject of County Lines and Child Criminal Exploitation.

Phil studied literature at the University of York, graduating in 2001.

A 17 year career with the police exposed him to the personal accounts and experiences of criminally exploited children and domestic abuse.

His writing – in both the fictional and non-fictional context - is motivated by a need to challenge and educate while providing an engaging and compelling experience for the audience or reader.

Phil cites numerous literary figures as being important and influential including Walt Whitman, J.B. Priestley, Virginia Woolf, T.S. Eliot and Chinua Achebe.

Copyright © 2022 Subversive Media Publications

All rights reserved. No part of this publication may be reproduced, distributed or transmitted in any form or by any means, including photocopying, recording or other electronic or mechanical methods without the prior written permission of the publisher, except in the case of brief quotations embodied in critical reviews and certain other non-commercial uses permitted by copyright law. For permission requests please email the publisher address:

"Attention: Permissions Coordinator" at the following address

team@inclusiuve-development.co.uk

Publisher's Cataloguing-in-Publication data:

Huckle, Natalia & Priestley, Phil: The Evil That We Do / Natalia Huckle Phil Priestley

ISBN: 97818382131-9-0

1. Main category of the publication – fiction
2. Other category – drama
3. Fiction – Fantasy/Urban

First edition.

www.ingramcontent.com/pod-product-compliance
Lightning Source LLC
Chambersburg PA
CBHW030103240426
43661CB00039B/1473/J